Also published by

Days in the Lives of Social Workers: 50 Professionals Tell "Real-Life" Stories from Social Work Practice

Guide to Selecting and Applying to Master of Social Work Programs

Improving Quality and Performance in Your Nonprofit Organization

The Nonprofit Handbook

The Nonprofit Internet Handbook

The Nonprofit Organization's Guide to E-Commerce

The Pennsylvania Nonprofit Handbook

The Social Worker's Internet Handbook

Why Is My Baby Crying: The 7-Minute Program for Soothing the Fussy Baby

Welcome to Methadonia

A Social Worker's Candid Account of Life in a Methadone Clinic

Rachel Greene Baldino, MSW, LCSW

White Hat Communications

Welcome to Methadonia
A Social Worker's Candid Account of Life in a Methadone Clinic

by Rachel Greene Baldino, MSW, LCSW

Published by:

White Hat Communications

P.O. Box 5390
Harrisburg, PA 17110-0390
717-238-3787 (voice)
717-238-2090 (fax)

The information in this volume is not intended as a substitute for consultation with health care professionals. Each individual's health concerns should be evaluated by a qualified professional.

Note: Names and identities of people mentioned in this book have been changed to protect their privacy, in accordance with professional standards of confidentiality.

Library of Congress Cataloging-in-Publication Data

Baldino, Rachel Greene, 1967-
  Welcome to methadonia : a social worker's candid account of
life in a methadone clinic / Rachel Greene Baldino.
    p. cm.
Includes index.
  ISBN 1-929109-02-4
  1. Heroin habit—Treatment—United States. 2. Methadone
maintenance—United States. 3. Social work with narcotic
addicts—United States. 4. Narcotic addicts—Rehabilitation—United
States. I. Title.
  HV5822.H4 B35 2000
  362.29'36'0973—dc21   00-009137

Table of Contents

For my parents,
Robert and Judith Greene,
my brother, Sean Greene,
and my husband,
Michael Baldino

Acknowledgments

To my editor and publisher, Linda Grobman, I would like to express my deepest gratitude for believing in me and supporting my writing efforts from the beginning.

I am also indebted to JoAnne Donato-Popko, MSW, LSW, MAC, James J. Korsog, MSW, and Jerry E. Lowery, MSW, for reviewing my manuscript and offering their invaluable suggestions.

In addition, I would like to thank my former colleagues and clients for teaching me so much, and my talented professors at the Boston College Graduate School of Social Work, particularly Professors Robert Castignola, Tom O'Hare, and Linda Sanford, for their wisdom and ability to inspire.

For their boundless generosity, insight, and spirit, I would also like to thank my wonderful writing teachers, Melanie Rae Thon, and in memoriam, Andre Dubus.

Finally, I would like to offer my love and thanks to my family and friends for encouraging me and keeping the faith no matter what. In particular, I would like to thank my four grandparents, none of whom lived to see the publication of this book, but all of whom are with me always in my heart.

Photo of author: Bachrach Photographers
Cover art: John Foxx Images

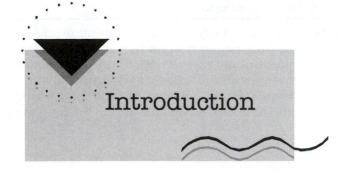

Introduction

I worked as a substance abuse counselor in a methadone clinic for one year, from November 1997 through November 1998, and it took me a good four or five months to become fully acclimated to the job. In this book, I discuss my former clients in general terms, but refrain from mentioning the psychological details of specific individuals out of respect for their privacy. The content of their innermost thoughts is their property, and theirs alone. Likewise, I do not reveal the names of my clients or my colleagues, or even the name of the agency or the city in which I worked. My main goal is to convey exactly what it felt like—day in and day out—to sit in a stuffy, windowless office with human beings who were suffering from a unique and devastating form of soul-sickness.

In social work school, my classmates and I often talked about how much we wanted to read some firsthand accounts of how it feels to be a new social worker. Of course, we read a great number of clinical descriptions of fieldwork, but we were hungry for something more personal and accessible. In these pages, I hope I have given readers exactly that: the "inside scoop" on how it feels to work as a new methadone counselor.

In retrospect, I believe that if I had read some personal accounts about working in the methadone field, I probably would have opted to work in a different clinical setting. Of course, mine is only one story, and every substance abuse counselor's experience is unique, but I hope that what I learned on the job can be of use to social work students, social workers, and anyone with an interest in substance abuse treatment, sociology, psychology, or public policy issues.

This account is meant to be much more than just a treatise on "vicarious traumatization." It is also intended to be a celebration of my former clients' strength and resilience. My job as a methadone counselor forced me to examine at close range precisely what can happen to human beings who have reached the breaking point. But my experiences at the clinic also taught me that it is entirely possible for people to emerge from the depths of despair to become whole, productive, and emotionally balanced individuals. And for that invaluable life lesson, I am eternally grateful.

Welcome to "Methadonia"

Methadonia—as some of the clients had nicknamed the clinic—is an unusual place. It is filled with people whose paths I may never have crossed had I not served as their social worker. In my mind's eye, I can still see the faces of each one of my clients, and I am sure that those faces will remain etched in my memory forever. Certain images and experiences are so indelible that they actually grow more vivid and powerful with the passage of time.

If you have ever seen someone laughing and joking and brimming with life one minute, and then high on heroin the next, you have some idea of how disturbing it can be to spend an extended period of time with opiate addicts. Heroin reduces vibrant, alive people to rubble, to empty shells. The metamorphosis is a terrifying thing to behold.

References to drug use abound in our culture. Think of the hallucinogenic moments in *Alice in Wonderland*, or the scene from *The Wizard of Oz* when Dorothy and her friends swoon from opium fumes in a lush field of swaying red poppies. That drug-induced stupor is what heroin addicts call "nodding out," and the fact that such a scene appears in one of the most famous children's movies ever made shows how pervasive drug allusions are in our society.

Before I took the job at the clinic, I had entertained the deluded notion that the clinic would be filled with bohemians, rebels, anarchists, and would-be rock stars. Needless to say, that turned out not to be the case. (Speaking of *The Wizard of Oz*, from the moment I set foot in the clinic, I knew that I was "not in Kansas anymore.") Most of the clients were impoverished, which is not to say that rich rock stars do not become heroin addicts (because we know that some of them do). Wealthy rock star addicts, however, usually go to luxurious, spa-style facilities for their treatment, not to state-subsidized methadone clinics. The role of "rebellious rock star" may indeed be the part that hardcore street addicts can least afford to play.

For ethical reasons, I have tried to keep the physical description of the clinic somewhat generic. I do, however, want to provide—at least in broad strokes—a sense of the sights and sounds of a methadone clinic. In terms of the way the clients dressed, a lot of the younger women who were actively prostituting dressed rather scantily, especially in the summertime. They wore short shorts or ultra-mini skirts, and they used dramatic, colorful makeup. The pimps wore flashy jewelry and outfits, while the rest of the male clients favored jeans, T-shirts, baseball caps, and work boots or sneakers. Of course, those of our clients who worked in offices or in stores wore standard business attire.

The counselors were expected to dress in that "casual-professional" mode that is so prevalent in offices nowadays. This policy distinguished the clinic from some of the more "grass roots" social service agencies I have visited since, where the counselors tend to dress very casually as a show of solidarity with their clients who cannot afford to buy fancy clothes.

The building that housed the clinic was an old, attractive brownstone with high, rather grand ceilings. The counseling area was located on one of the upper floors, and each counselor had a private office. (Obviously, cubicles would not have been conducive to client confidentiality.) Most of the counselors decorated their offices with bright, cheery prints; and in the common areas, a large number of colorful "Just say no" posters filled the walls.

Unlike the counseling floor, the first floor, where the dosing clinic was located, had much more of a medical office feel. There was a waiting area and a reception desk and, of course, the dosing window, which was locked with a thick, steel door. The clients walked up to the window, where a nurse prepared and handed each of them a mixture of Tang® and methadone in a paper cup. The security guards checked client identification cards and made sure that no one got too unruly. There were usually a few minor skirmishes per week, and on occasion, the guards had to break up fist fights. Our clients said that the metha-done/Tang® mixture tasted so rancid and bitter that they some-times had trouble keeping it down.

No description of a methadone clinic would be complete with-out some mention of the police presence, both real and imag-ined, in the adjacent area. According to our clients, police offic-ers were lurking everywhere. I was somewhat inclined to believe them. Our clients seemed to have developed a sort of built-in "police radar" as a result of all their run-ins with law enforce-ment over the years. For instance, there was a great deal of construction going on a few blocks away, so there were always construction workers milling about in front of the clinic. After a while, the clients had convinced themselves that half of the men wandering around in hard hats were actually undercover police officers in the process of setting up some kind of a massive sting. (No such sting ever took place, at least during my tenure.) These same clients were also certain that several of the businessmen and women who drove by the clinic were actually members of yet another fleet of undercover police driving around in unmarked cars.

In our clients' defense, while they may have been exaggerat-ing, I believe there were a number of undercover police officers in the neighborhood. I say this because periodically an angry client would come charging into the clinic having just been "shaken down" (that is, randomly stopped and searched) by an out-of-uniform officer.

As was true of several of my fellow counselors, I had come to the job from a sheltered, middle-class, suburban background. Consequently, the "culture shock" I experienced at the begin-ning was intense. The drug culture is a universe unto itself, complete with its own secret laws and hidden agendas, and I often felt like an unwelcome stranger in a foreign land. Not sur-prisingly, I also had difficulty readjusting to "civilian life" after a full year in the trenches of the so-called "war on drugs."

Some of the clients went out of their way to underscore the differences between us. They inquired with great curiosity about my "college girl" diction, my lack of a regional accent, my "preppy" taste in clothes, and even the way I carried myself. A few of them came right out and asked if I "came from money." In the greater scheme of things, I am no rich girl; but in comparison with poverty-stricken methadone clients, I suppose I am. In essence, the clients spoke out loud about the class differences that many people notice but are afraid to mention in polite society. Their brazen candor and lack of self-censorship were fascinating—even refreshing at times—but also contributed to my ever-growing sense of malaise.

Sadly, there were times when the clients' combination of curiosity and candor dissolved into pure rancor. But class conflict was the source of only half of the tension that existed between the staff and the clients; trauma was the source of the other half. My colleagues and I had grown up loved and nurtured by our parents, whereas many of our clients had not. Moreover, a large number of the clients had experienced, or witnessed, or perpetrated the kind of horrendous atrocities that we had only read about in newspapers. My clients were only too aware of just how treacherous a place the world can be, while I was still harboring the illusion that it is generally safe and benign. Frankly, I think that I would have preferred to go on living in a state of "ignorant bliss," but my methadone clients simply would not let me. They insisted on teaching me the true meaning of despair.

Prior to working as a methadone counselor, I had always thought of myself as very broad-minded. You can imagine, then, how unnerving it was to discover just how narrow-minded I could become when "backed up against the wall," so to speak. When my clients were working diligently on their sobriety, I was content to blame society for their suffering. However, when they were screaming at me or frightening me—as some of them were prone to do rather often—I sometimes gave in to the terrible temptation to blame the clients themselves for their difficulties. Before I was verbally assaulted by some of my methadone clients, I never thought I could "blame the victim" like that, and I am not at all proud of the ambivalent, resentful feelings that the job occasionally brought out in me. On the other hand, it is vitally important to discuss these matters openly.

A more seasoned counselor would probably have known better than to take the verbal pummeling of understandably embittered methadone clients quite so personally. However, I was hampered by my inexperience, as well as my hypersensitivity. I was also still learning how to put exactly enough clinical distance between my clients' suffering and myself.

In essence, methadone treatment is "opiate replacement therapy" for individuals who are physically dependent on heroin.

That is to say, heroin, which is an illicit opiate, is replaced in the addict's system by methadone, a legally prescribed opiate. One of the benefits of substituting methadone for heroin is that addicts do not have to endure the excruciatingly painful process of withdrawing from heroin "cold turkey."

Yet, I found that in some cases methadone inflicts nearly as much damage on an opiate addict's life as illicit drugs. Just as the clients' lives had once revolved around procuring heroin, their lives now revolved around going to the methadone clinic every day. Consequently, our clients still viewed themselves as "slaves" to a drug. In fact, they believed the only difference was that they now had a new "master": methadone.

While working at the clinic, I felt by turns compassionate, furious, disgusted, frustrated, hurt, inspired, intrigued, terrified, amused, depressed, elated, bamboozled, betrayed, enlightened, and more. If you can name the emotion, I can honestly say that I felt it at one point or another. Methadone counselors can experience the entire gamut of human emotions in a single day.

Typically, end-stage heroin addicts are people who have lost everything—their jobs, familial relationships, possessions, pride, and self-respect—all as a direct result of heroin addiction. When the craving for heroin takes over, it shuts out all reason and common sense. Thoughts of the drug become pervasive, and addicts need to use greater and greater quantities of it just to get a minimal high. There can never be enough heroin.

Even those heroin addicts who are disciplined and focused in other areas of their lives find it extremely difficult to shake heroin addiction. This is because opiate dependence is not only psychological and emotional in nature, but it is physical as well. And it is the physical dimension of opiate addiction that makes it virtually impervious to will power. Sadly, suicide becomes an alluring option to some heroin addicts, because it can seem to them to be the only way to break out of the vicious cycle.

When people think of "walking heroin casualties," they often picture people who came of age during the sixties. After all, this was the era when drug experimentation as an adolescent rite of passage bubbled up out of the counterculture and spilled over into the mainstream. Most of the hardcore drug addicts who grew up in the sixties have little to show for their years of hard living other than pain and regret. Nevertheless, many young people continue to look back on the free love, "anything goes" spirit of that era with a sense of vicarious liberation and romantic nostalgia. I believe this is one reason why some young people continue to turn to heroin and other drugs in the first place.

Addicts attempt to cope with their emotional pain by obliterating it. Certainly there are times when we all feel the urge to escape from the pressures of daily living. For many non-addicts, however, it is enough of a stress reliever to take a hot bath, read a trashy novel, or relax in front of a mindless movie. Also, non-addicts can enjoy an occasional cocktail without fearing that alcohol consumption will take over their lives. However, for the hardcore heroin addict, escape means zoning out to the point of total oblivion. The chase for heroin quickly takes on a life of its own, spiraling out of control, and pushing everything else—family, work, the experience of genuine human emotions—to the sidelines.

I wish I could debunk the mythology that has grown up around heroin addicts over the years. I wish, for instance, that I could tell you that the stereotype of the "spaced-out" heroin addict is a total falsehood; sadly, I cannot. This unfortunate image actually represents a significant percentage of methadone clients, and it would be disingenuous of me to pretend otherwise. Some methadone clients never achieve sobriety; they can be seen wandering down darkened city streets in a sort of purgatorial fog.

A fair number of clients at the clinic confessed that they would stop at nothing to get money for drugs. The most common criminal activities were prostituting, mugging, hustling, burglarizing, pimping, dealing, shoplifting and even ticket scalping. I must admit that after working with such damaged (and, in some cases, dangerous) people, my colleagues and I experienced a fair amount of what clinicians call "vicarious traumatization."

Fortunately, I also worked with clients who threw themselves into their quest for sobriety. During treatment, they stopped taking all illegal drugs. They started to pick up the pieces of their ravaged lives and careers, and to mend their relationships with family members and friends. There were not many of these "success stories" at the clinic, but there were enough of them to give my colleagues and me a sense of hope.

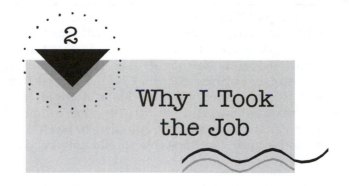

Why I Took the Job

After I graduated from social work school, filled with all the usual dreams of "saving the world," I started looking in the "Help Wanted" section of the newspaper. I immediately noticed that there were a number of job openings in the substance abuse field. (The sheer abundance of such vacancies should have been my first warning that perhaps these were among the hardest-to-fill positions.) At the time, I was so eager for my first bona fide professional counseling job that I was oblivious to even the most obvious clues.

The position I applied for at the clinic had been advertised as a generic "substance abuse counselor" job. There was no indication in the ad copy that the position was at a methadone clinic. Perhaps if there had been, I would not have applied for the job at all. I wonder how surprised I must have looked when the interviewer eventually broke the news to me that this site was in fact a methadone clinic. At that point, my only frame of reference was a scene from the movie *Sid and Nancy* when the actors who play punk rocker Sid Vicious and his girlfriend Nancy Spungeon walk up to a methadone dosing window in New York City, and someone hands each of them a little paper cup filled with juice. With that image in my head, I tried to figure out exactly what I would be doing with these clients. Would I be handing out little Dixie cups of Tang®? (No, that is the exclusive domain of the nursing staff. Methadone is a controlled substance, which means that it can only be dispensed by qualified medical personnel.)

The most memorable thing about that interview is that I was told I would get "a lot of counseling experience with both individuals and groups." This was music to my ears. Until then, the interviews I'd had were for "case management" jobs. Case managers get a great deal of experience with assessment and referral work, but only rarely do they get the chance to engage in long-term therapy with their clients. I had assumed that case management jobs were the only kind I would qualify for fresh out of social work school, and yet this program administrator was telling me that I was already qualified to work as a full-fledged psychotherapist. (Perhaps this should have been another red flag for me.)

As with many social work jobs, the salary was relatively low, but I had emotionally prepared myself for that. Luckily, the other counselors I met seemed friendly and welcoming, though I could tell that they thought I was pretty naïve. They were absolutely right—I was as green as they come. And I certainly had no idea what I was getting myself into by accepting this job offer.

What first struck me when the interviewer took me on a tour of the clinic was that the pain in the air was thick and palpable. On any given day, in any given methadone clinic across the country, you might encounter an HIV-positive man discussing his fourth bout of double pneumonia in a six-month period. Or you might overhear another young man talking about discovering his roommate dead of an overdose in the bathtub. Or you might eavesdrop on a woman discussing her eviction from a rat-infested apartment—an eviction for which she has little recourse because of all the drug possession and prostitution charges on her police record. If there is indeed a "war on drugs" going on in America today, then I would argue that methadone clients are caught right in the crossfire.

After a few weeks on the job, what became just as palpable as the clients' pain was the inner strength they could summon in the face of crushing odds. Ultimately, their strength seemed even more unfathomable than their suffering. How could people who had been so shattered by life muster the courage and stamina required simply to go on living? What mysterious spiritual or moral resources had they managed to tap into, despite the cruel hand they had been dealt by the fates?

3

Heroin Addiction

Heroin is derived from morphine, which is a natural substance extracted from the seeds of poppies. It comes in three different forms: white powder, brown powder, or a dark, sticky clump, known as "black tar heroin." Heroin is generally "cut" or combined with other powders, such as sugar or starch. Unfortunately, some dealers also cut heroin with poisons like strychnine or bleach.

For users, one of the greatest dangers of purchasing heroin nowadays is the unpredictably high purity level. Dealers still cut or dilute their heroin supply with other substances, but they often include more pure heroin in each batch. Therefore, every time heroin users inject the drug into their veins, they run the risk of either overdosing on heroin that is too pure, or poisoning themselves with any number of the toxic substances the drug may have been "cut" with, such as rat poison.

Heroin has to be dissolved in heated liquid (usually water) before it can be drawn into a syringe and injected. Some of the more cautious heroin users draw the liquefied drug into the syringe through a very small piece of a cigarette filter, in order to sift out as many toxins and impurities as possible. Many addicts, however, do not filter their heroin before use.

According to the National Institute of Drug Abuse's (NIDA) *Research Report, Heroin Abuse and Addiction: NIH Publication No. 97-4165*, the number of new heroin users has steadily increased since 1992. Most alarmingly, the number of first-time heroin users between the ages of twelve and seventeen increased by 400% from the 1980s to 1995.

The same NIDA *Research Report* states that the typical intravenous heroin user injects the drug four times a day. When users inject heroin, the time between injection and the onset of euphoria is only seven or eight seconds, whereas the effects from smoking or snorting heroin are generally not felt for ten to fifteen minutes. All three forms of heroin use are highly addictive.

Shortly after an individual injects heroin, the drug travels from the bloodstream to the brain, where it changes into morphine and binds to the opioid receptors. At this moment, many users experience a "rush." The fact that heroin travels to the brain so quickly to produce an almost instantaneous euphoric effect is one of the features that makes it extremely addictive. During this initial rush, many users experience facial flushing, dry mouth, a heavy sensation in their hands and feet, nausea, vomiting, and itchiness.

Some heroin addicts are so fond of the rush that they use a technique commonly referred to as "booting," in which they inject a little heroin into the vein, pull some of their own blood back into the syringe, inject a little more of this mixed fluid, pull a little more blood back into the syringe, inject some more into the vein, and so on. This activity induces a series of smaller, but still potent rushes, as opposed to a single, larger one.

Once the rush wears off, most users slip into a barely conscious state known on the streets as a "nod." During this phase of the intoxication, users feel sleepy, often for several hours. Their thinking becomes clouded, because the heroin suppresses their entire central nervous system. Their cardiac and respiratory activities slow down considerably, in some cases to the point of death.

Many of our clients at the clinic stated that they felt more addicted to the so-called "nodding" portion of heroin intoxication than to the initial rush, which is relatively brief. During a heroin-induced nod, they explained that they felt they were taking a "mental vacation" from their own lives, worries, fears, and pain. For many users, heroin represents the "Great Escape," because it temporarily destroys one's capacity to think at the abstract level.

I heard one heroin user describe the sensation of "nodding out" like this: "When I'm high on heroin, I feel like I'm on the same level as my cat. My cat never worries about his parents' health, or his kids' grades, or money problems, or being lonely. My cat just sits around eating, sleeping, and being a cat. And of course, my cat never worries about dying. And the thing is, when I'm high on heroin, neither do I." It is this sensation of limbo-like nothingness, the total absence of thought, feeling, fear, and anxiety (including the ability to temporarily "forget" about one's own mortality), that is so appealing to so many heroin users.

To summarize briefly, the short-term effects of heroin use, according to the aforementioned NIDA *Research Report* on heroin addiction, include an initial rush of euphoria, followed by "de-pressed respiration, clouded mental functioning, nausea and vomiting, and suppression of pain." In the case of pregnant women, heroin use can also cause miscarriages. The authors of the same NIDA report further explain that long-term heroin abuse can have serious consequences, such as severe chronic medical conditions. These conditions include "addiction, infectious dis-eases like HIV/AIDS and hepatitis B and C, collapsed veins, bacterial infections, abscesses, infection of the heart lining and valves, arthritis and other rheumatologic problems."

The NIDA report also states: "Addiction is a chronic, relaps-ing disease, characterized by compulsive drug seeking and use and by neurochemical and molecular changes in the brain." When people become addicted to heroin, using the drug becomes their primary purpose in life. Because of the chronic, progres-sive nature of opioid addiction, users eventually become physi-cally dependent on heroin and experience severe withdrawal symptoms if they are denied access to the drug. Usually, these withdrawal symptoms, which include insomnia, diarrhea, nau-sea, muscle and bone pain, and cold flashes, dissipate after a few days.

Even after the physical withdrawal symptoms subside, how-ever, many addicts continue to experience powerful emotional and psychological cravings for heroin. While withdrawal from heroin is generally not fatal to adults in relatively good health, it can—and often does—kill the fetuses of pregnant heroin users. Also, those pregnant users who do not lose their babies to heroin run the risk of delivering very prematurely. According to the NIDA report, the children of heroin addicts are significantly more susceptible to Sudden Infant Death Syndrome, or SIDS. In ad-dition, intravenous drug users now comprise the fastest grow-ing segment of the HIV-positive population in the United States.

Regarding the various forms of treatment available to heroin abusers, methadone treatment has been employed in the treatment of opioid dependence for over thirty years. When clients are taking the correct dose of methadone, they feel neither intoxicated nor sedated. They are able to drive, work, and concentrate on complex tasks. Methadone suppresses heroin withdrawal symptoms, allowing clients to function without feeling sick. Provided they are not simultaneously abusing illicit drugs, people on methadone are able to experience all of life's joys and pains. Their emotions are not numbed, but their physical cravings for heroin are suppressed. The problem with methadone for some clients is that they are afraid of feeling true emotions because they have grown deeply attached to the numbness, or absence of emotion, that they experience on heroin.

Some treatment facilities use an alternative synthetic substance called LAAM, or levo-alpha-acetyl-methadol, instead of methadone. LAAM stays in the system for up to seventy-two hours, unlike methadone, which is metabolized in twenty-four to thirty-six hours. I will discuss LAAM programs at greater length in the final chapter of this book.

Naloxone and naltrexone are substances that have been found to block the pleasurable effects of heroin. The authors of the NIDA report point out that these two medications are most effective with "highly motivated" individuals. Also, scientists are continuing to research the efficacy of other opiate-blocking agents, such as buprenorphine.

Before beginning any kind of long-term treatment for opioid dependence, most users enter detoxification facilities to withdraw from heroin, and other drugs, under a doctor's supervision, often with the assistance of certain medications that alleviate the symptoms of opiate withdrawal. In detoxification facilities (usually located on specially designated floors of hospitals), clients are denied access to any illicit drugs. The detoxification process usually lasts for several days, depending on the amount of heroin the individual client has been using. It is critical to emphasize that, by itself, physical detoxification is not a sufficient treatment for heroin addiction. It needs to be followed by an intensive inpatient or outpatient program, such as residential or methadone treatment.

At the clinic, when clients were having difficulty complying with the requirements of the methadone program, we often referred them to long-term residential programs, where they were supervised around the clock. Some clients felt they could not trust themselves to stay clean and sober without this kind of intensive, twenty-four-hour-a-day supervision.

There are various models of inpatient, residential programs for heroin addicts. Some residential programs last one month, while others last three months or longer. Medicaid covers many of these programs, some of which target specific sub-populations within the heroin-using populace, such as pregnant women, women with small children, or HIV-positive individuals. The great strength of residential treatment is that the inpatient care providers are able to immerse their participants in sobriety counseling morning, noon, and night.

Our clients who had utilized residential treatment at one time or another often talked about how powerful and effective it can be to participate in a sobriety group right after breakfast, another after lunch, one before dinner, and yet another after dinner. On one hand, it can be emotionally and physically exhausting to participate in so many group therapy sessions. But on the other hand, it can also be a wonderful way to absorb and fully process information about sobriety, and then put that information to work in one's own life. Some clients who "graduate" from residential programs then opt (or are court-mandated) to live in a halfway house, often for six months or more before returning home. This allows clients to accumulate sober time while slowly making the transition back into living in the community.

Cognitive-behavioral therapy is used in both outpatient and inpatient heroin treatment programs. According to NIDA's report on heroin use, the best treatment for opioid dependence is usually some combination of pharmacological treatment and "talk therapy." Cognitive-behavioral techniques, in which clients are taught first how to identify and alter destructive thinking patterns, and then how to develop healthy coping skills, have been especially successful in helping recovering heroin addicts to continue on the road to sobriety.

What is important is to tailor each treatment plan to suit the needs of each individual client. For instance, if a methadone client is struggling with some of the compliance issues integral to this outpatient treatment model, it is vital for that client's treatment providers to consider a residential program as a viable alternative. Each client's treatment needs are different, and each client's needs evolve over the course of time. Thus, it is crucial for substance abuse treatment providers to remain flexible and open to change in caring for their clients.

4

Getting In: The Intake Interview

I once thought that all a person needed to do in order to be admitted to a methadone clinic was to show up with track marks on his or her arms. As I discovered, however, there was a long, involved screening process, and no one was guaranteed automatic admission. Potential clients could not just walk in the front door and expect to be interviewed. For example, at the clinic where I worked, some of our referrals came from hospitals, detoxification facilities, and the van drivers for the local needle exchange program. Our waiting list was always very long, because there were only so many treatment openings and the demand for these openings was great. Also, the clinic census, or the total number of clients in treatment at any given time, could never exceed 250. We did not have enough resources or personnel to accommodate more than this number of clients.

Clients had to wait six weeks or longer to be granted an "intake" interview. In fact, they had to lobby very hard just to get an interview. Lobbying involved calling the receptionist each week at a designated time to remind her that they were out on the streets abusing drugs, and in dire straits. Since people who call methadone clinics are invariably desperate, you can imagine how torturous it must have been for our clients to wait six weeks to be granted an interview, with absolutely no guarantee of admission to the clinic. A single day can feel like an eternity when people are desperate and have finally admitted to themselves that they are in need of serious help.

Many substance abuse counselors and addicts alike regard methadone as the treatment of "last resort," largely because it involves switching opiate-addicted individuals from one addictive substance to another. For this reason, many of the intake candidates I interviewed did not want to be on methadone. However, they had not been successful with any other forms of treatment, such as the inpatient detoxification programs or the highly structured residential settings mentioned in the previous chapter. Further, many of our clients despised methadone so intensely because it made them feel as if they were trapped in a sort of limbo, or at the last bleak way station on a long, arduous journey to Hell.

Most of our clients had volunteered to enter methadone treatment, but some had been ordered to do so by a judge as a condition of their probation. Probation officers had the right to call the clinic staff to make sure that their clients were complying with all of the clinic's rules and regulations. Regardless of whether clients had been court-ordered to enter treatment or had entered treatment voluntarily, all of them were then mandated by the clinic administration to take part in every aspect of methadone treatment, including weekly individual counseling, weekly group counseling, and urinalysis.

After waiting six or more weeks for their intake interview, potential clients still had several additional hurdles to clear before they could enter treatment. For starters, applicants who were too high to answer questions were automatically turned away. The clinical staff operated on the assumption that a treatment candidate who could not manage to make a strong first impression would probably not be a successful client over the long haul. Also, if treatment candidates were too agitated to provide urine samples, they were asked to re-interview on another day. Because of the enormous weight given urinalysis during the course of treatment, candidates who could not urinate upon request did not stand a good chance of being admitted to the program.

Because I was a novice, I made my share of poor judgment calls. For instance, I met with a few candidates who initially seemed focused, but who rapidly disintegrated before my eyes during the interview. Before working at the clinic, I had never seen people "nod out" like that. It was almost as if they were suffering from narcolepsy. They would literally fall asleep in the middle of a sentence, only to wake up a few seconds later to finish the sentence, as if nothing had happened.

The intake session itself involved a lengthy, comprehensive interview process in which candidates were asked all sorts of deeply personal questions about their psychiatric, medical, professional, and substance abuse histories. After conducting these interviews, we counselors wrote summaries that we presented to one another in staff meetings for collective consideration. It must have been extremely difficult for the treatment candidates to disclose all those personal details to complete strangers, especially when these strangers had so much control over their destinies.

The following is a typical (though fictitious) intake presentation: "John Doe is a 42-year-old, unmarried, Catholic poly-substance abuser of Irish and French-Canadian descent. His main 'drugs of choice' are heroin and alcohol. Mr. Doe resides on Brown Street with his mother, and he intravenously uses 15-20 bags of heroin per day. He is on Medicaid, and he works intermittently in factory jobs. Between jobs, he supports his drug habit by collecting and selling scrap metal, and also by dealing, begging, borrowing, and stealing. He completed the eighth grade and earned his GED in prison at age 32. Mr. Doe has been incarcerated twice, both times for breaking and entering. He is currently on probation for a heroin possession charge, and he signed consent forms giving the clinic staff permission to speak to his probation officer. He has chronic, non-active hepatitis B, and he stated that at present he is HIV-negative and that he gets retested every six months. Currently, he does not have a primary care physician, but he understands that he will need to acquire one if he is accepted for methadone treatment. Mr. Doe denied any psychiatric history, and he said he has no problems with anger, violence, or impulse control. Regarding his presentation: he was neatly groomed, his affect was flat, his speech pattern was slow; his hands were shaky, and his voice was soft. He also mentioned that he was in pain during the interview because he was withdrawing from both heroin and alcohol."

This client profile is typical in that it presents the picture of a man who never really managed to "kick-start" his adult life. Many of the clients lived at home with their mothers, and had never married or had families of their own, just like "Mr. John Doe." That said, however, I should also point out that the skeletal facts of Mr. Doe's sad existence tell us very little about what he was really like as a human being. We have a sense of his demographic profile, yet we have no real sense of his individuality, his essence. We know, for instance, that he dropped out of school in the eighth grade—a tragedy in its own right. But we do not know from this abbreviated portrait why he stopped going to school at that particular time. By reducing the tragic life stories of individuals to these laundry lists of dry statistics, I suspect that we clinicians were trying to transform flesh-and-blood human beings in need of treatment into math problems in need of solving. If we had considered each tragic story in non-clinical terms, we probably would have been buried under the weight of sorrow and human misery. There were times, however, when I believe we concealed our clients' humanity all too well from ourselves, because we certainly ended up rejecting many treatment candidates.

In fact, more than half of the suffering souls who participated in the intake process were turned away. For example, if candidates could not document a lengthy substance abuse treatment history—including multiple stays in detoxification facilities—they were automatically rejected for not having exhausted other treatment options.

Candidates could also be turned away if they had no means of paying for treatment, which raises a very sticky ethical issue. Private insurance companies are reluctant to pay for methadone maintenance treatment, mainly because it is costly and can continue for the duration of a patient's lifetime. Thus, even when heroin addicts have steady full-time jobs with basic benefits including medical coverage, generally they do not have the right to utilize that health insurance to cover the cost of methadone treatment. They must pay for drug treatment on their own, out of pocket (albeit on a sliding scale). In other words, in our current system, working heroin addicts with health insurance are often ineligible for methadone treatment coverage. Conversely, the unemployed, the uninsured, and the underinsured have access to "free" methadone treatment, although of course it is not truly free. It is actually paid for by Medicaid and the state's Department of Public Health.

The subliminal—and I believe classist—message that this sends to potential methadone clients is that they should not seek legitimate employment offering health insurance if they want treatment. In other words, to obtain drug treatment, they should remain unemployed, uninsured, outside the mainstream, and inside the underclass. I would contend, then, that private insurers contribute to the vicious cycle of poverty and drug addiction when they refuse to provide coverage for methadone treatment. I am not arguing that methadone treatment is perfect; it is not. Methadone treatment is, however, one of but a few viable treatment modalities currently available to opiate addicts. It is therefore inhumane and discriminatory for private insurers not to cover methadone treatment, if not in full, then at least in part.

The desperation of our intake candidates was unbearable to behold. Time and again, they recited some variation on the theme: "I would not wish heroin addiction on my worst enemy's dog." They did wish that they had never laid eyes on heroin. And they would have given anything to turn back the hands of time and make different choices. When they tried to recall why they had experimented with heroin in the first place, they usually described the hubris and sense of invincibility that many teenagers possess to one degree or another. That is to say, they honestly believed that, among all their friends, they would be the only ones who would be able to try heroin without getting hooked. Somehow, they would be able to use it once or twice—just enough to experience that "better-than-orgasmic" high that they had heard so much about—without feeling compelled to use it again. They had been curious, and they had fallen prey to their own adolescent bravado. But—initially, at least—this was their only real crime. Now, as adults, they were paying a very high price for the bad choices they had made as youngsters. A few fleeting moments of pleasure had resulted in a lifetime of torment for themselves and their families. The punishment hardly seems to fit the crime.

Not all of the intake clients had grown up poor, abused, and undereducated (though many of them had). The one trait that all our treatment candidates had in common was self-loathing. Without exception, they despised themselves for the destruction they had caused, both in their own lives and in the lives of those they loved. I have never seen as much self-hatred as I did when I looked into the eyes of those treatment candidates. One of the questions that appeared on the standardized questionnaire we used with all of the potential clients was: "What are your strengths?" A few people could manage to come up with one or two mildly positive points about themselves. However, most of them said they had absolutely no redeeming qualities, and that they did not deserve to go on living.

To complicate matters even further, as much as the clients hated themselves for trying heroin in the first place, they also felt deeply nostalgic for that very first time they had ever gotten high. That first experience with heroin was something many of them described as a million times better than the best sexual experience they had ever had. The trouble was that every high after that initial taste of bliss paled by comparison. Still, each time they injected or snorted heroin, they prayed in vain to recapture that initial, blinding rush of euphoria.

What was most disturbing about the intake interviews was that these individuals were pleading with their intake counselors—quite literally begging us—for their lives. They wanted their sobriety, to be sure. But what they wanted even more was some relief from the "drug chase," a chase that included an endless cycle of hustling, prostituting, dealing, and stealing. Despite all of its drawbacks, to these desperate souls, methadone treatment represented a final chance to step off that treadmill.

Every week in our staff meetings, I advocated as strongly as I could on behalf of my intake clients, mainly because I could not bear the thought of turning away even a single desperate candidate. And yet, as I noted earlier, only half of the potential clients we interviewed were admitted into treatment. Thus, for every person I had the opportunity to call with good news, I had to call another one with bad news. This terrible power was probably the aspect of the job I disliked the most. I hated making those phone calls of rejection, because I dreaded listening to the anguish in those voices at the other end of the line.

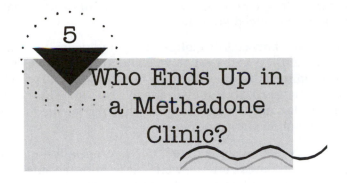

5

Who Ends Up in a Methadone Clinic?

I try not to over-generalize when it comes to heroin addicts. I must say, however, that after I conducted several intake sessions with treatment candidates, I did notice some common threads running through their lives. For example, the majority reported that they had begun taking drugs when they were still pre-teens. That was when many of them had started experimenting with marijuana, alcohol, glue sniffing, mushrooms, acid, or speed. Several had older siblings, neighborhood friends, or dealers who had "peer-pressured" them into trying various substances, and who had also provided them with drugs and alcohol on a regular basis.

Many of our clients had grown up in poverty, with parents or guardians who had been by turns abusive and neglectful. A fair number of our clients had grown up in foster care and had been moved repeatedly from one home to another. For as long as they could remember, they had felt unwanted and unloved. Consequently, as adults, they had no sense of emotional stability and they trusted no one.

Among those who had grown up in their biological families, a significant number reported that one or more of their relatives (parents, siblings, aunts and uncles, grandparents, and/or cousins) had also struggled with substance abuse. In other words, when they were young, they observed heavy drug and alcohol use in their home environments. They simply grew up copying behavior that they had come to view as normal. To them, getting high was just another part of life, as natural as eating or sleeping. It can be very difficult for a heroin addict to "unlearn" a form of learned behavior that is so deeply ingrained. On the other hand, drug counselors assume that this sort of behavior modification is indeed possible.

A handful of my clients claimed they had never been abused, that, in fact, they had been loved and nurtured as children. They also claimed that they had only become involved with heroin because they "liked" it. But even those who swore that they had never been damaged emotionally as children seemed to be suffering from some core emptiness.

Gradually—or, in some cases, not so gradually—most of the treatment candidates I interviewed had "graduated" in their later teens or early twenties from drinking binges and marijuana-smoking to snorting cocaine and/or heroin. The last step—using the needle—was something that a lot of them ended up doing still later. However, as their tolerance increased, there came a time when no amount of heroin used either nasally or intravenously could get them high. And when they stopped being able to get high, they had finally despaired and had sought treatment for the first time. One of the saddest features of heroin addiction, however, is that a person's initial course of treatment is rarely his last. Literally and figuratively, heroin gets "under your skin" like nothing else on earth.

By now, most people know that one of the ways HIV is spread is through the use of shared needles. Several strains of hepatitis—most notably hepatitis B and hepatitis C—are also blood-borne pathogens, which means that these viruses can also be spread by sharing dirty needles, as is the case with HIV. Hepatitis attacks the liver and causes several other health complications, such as edema, which in turn causes a dangerous level of fluid retention. Some of the clients at the clinic suffered from edema in their extremities, which caused their forearms and calves to swell to twice or three times their normal size.

There is a vaccination for the prevention of hepatitis B, but none as yet for hepatitis C. On the other hand, medical treatment (known as interferon treatment) is available for hepatitis C, which several clients at the clinic were undergoing. Some of them, however, found interferon treatment for hepatitis C to be nearly as debilitating as chemotherapy. Sadly, many of our clients had both HIV and hepatitis, which placed a double strain on their immune systems.

Our methadone clients seemed to be about three times as unlucky as the general population. When most people have negative experiences, those events tend to occur over a period of months or years. But because of their addiction issues coupled with their medical problems, methadone clients can frequently experience multiple devastating tragedies in the span of a few days. For example, a methadone client might have a heart attack on a Monday, lose his mother to cancer Tuesday, and have his parental rights revoked on Thursday.

As for our clients' mental health, many had been plagued by lifelong anxiety, or depression, or both. Also, a fair number suffered from more severe mental illnesses, such as bipolar disorder or paranoid schizophrenia. Still others had been diagnosed with Axis II disorders (discussed in Chapter 26), or pervasive "characterological" conditions, usually narcissistic personality disorder or borderline personality disorder.

In terms of their living situations, a handful of our clients had their own apartments or houses. As I mentioned in the last chapter, however, many of them—even those over forty—lived with their parents. More specifically, they lived with their mothers, because often their fathers were deceased or just out of their lives. By residing with their mothers well into adulthood, they could avoid leading any semblance of an adult life, which was a rather convenient arrangement. Because they did not have to pay for rent or utilities, they were free to spend all of their money on drugs. In other cases, clients had parents, partners, or siblings who wittingly or unwittingly aided and abetted them by giving them cash and/or a place to stay, so they would not have to turn to prostitution or dealing or stealing to obtain their drugs. In the substance abuse counseling field, this phenomenon is known as "enabling."

According to my more experienced colleagues, many of our clients were suffering from a collective case of arrested development because they had started abusing drugs when they were still very young, thereby stunting the natural maturation process. Indeed, many of our clients could be rather childlike in their behavior. For instance, whenever they bought new jeans or sneakers rather than spending money on drugs, they showed us their purchases. For once, they had exercised some self-control by buying something other than drugs, and they simply wanted to have their good conduct acknowledged by their counselors. These gestures were touching, but they were also indicative of our clients' stunted emotional growth.

Our clients often said they were accustomed to being treated unkindly. Strangers on the street gave them dirty looks. Family members belittled them on a regular basis. Even in their own doctors' offices, they said that the nurses were chatty and friendly until they learned that the clients were intravenous drug users, at which point they turned as cold as ice. Many of my clients told me that after enough people treated them as if they were worthless, they started to believe it themselves. Some clients enjoyed coming to the clinic because it was one of the few places where they were treated with kindness and respect.

In addition, many of our methadone clients had served time in prison. Some of them had been able to procure drugs behind bars, while others had not. Those who had not been able to obtain drugs in prison looked back on that time as a much-needed respite from the exhausting drug chase. Ironically, physical incarceration had liberated them from the emotional prison of drug abuse. Moreover, some of them liked the fact that prison was such a structured environment. In certain ways, they explained, being in jail was like living with their mothers. Prison could be quite frightening, to be sure, but in both settings they ate regularly and had warm beds and a roof over their heads. And in prison (as at Mother's house), they did not have to pay bills, nor did they have to do any of the other chores associated with being an adult. Not only was someone else in charge of feeding them and providing them with clothes, warmth, and shelter, but—in some cases at least—in prison someone else was also in charge of keeping them away from drugs. And according to my clients, sobriety is much easier to maintain if someone else is in charge.

Some of our clients had led what can best be characterized as a "transient" or "drifter" lifestyle. This generally involved staying with one friend until something bad happened, and then another, and then another, burning bridges all over town. They stole from their friends and family members, not out of malice, but because they had enormous drug habits to feed, habits that cost money. If active heroin addicts need to sell a friend's stereo system for cash, they might not allow anything—even friendship—to stand in the way.

Interestingly, the clients did not usually steal from the clinic. Once, a staff member had a wallet stolen from her office while she was on her lunch break. After that, we stopped taking our purses and wallets to work. Also, the clinic's VCR would vanish once in a while. To be truthful, I was surprised it did not disappear more often than it did. And right before I started working at the clinic, there had been a rash of clock-radio thefts, but that was about the extent of stealing at the clinic.

The client population at the clinic was not very diverse. There were a few Latino-Americans, African-Americans, and Asian-Americans, but the vast majority of the clients we served were white, perhaps because most of the residents of the neighborhood where the clinic was located were white. Regarding the socioeconomic status of the clients, there was also very little diversity. Most of the clients were poor, undereducated, and involved in one or more forms of criminal activity to support their drug habits.

While its racial and socioeconomic composition was relatively uniform, the client population was slightly more diverse in other areas. For instance, roughly half of our clients were female (which I gather is not the case at all clinics). One of the reasons we served so many female clients was that our clinic was focused on treating all heroin addicts, including pregnant women. Also, there were a fair number of gay and transgender clients at our clinic.

The clients ranged in age from twenty to seventy-five. When I first arrived, most of the clients were in their forties. However, during my final few months at the clinic, a "youth-quake" began shaking the very foundations of "Methadonia" with dramatic and unexpected force. These treatment candidates were young people who had already exhausted their other treatment options and were now desperate enough to try methadone. For a while, we counselors were "in denial" about these youngsters. We simply did not want to believe that they had gotten so deeply involved in drug abuse and addiction at such a young age. Therefore, we initially rejected many of these intake candidates based solely on their youth. We worried about these young people becoming enslaved to methadone at such a tender age. Also, we did not want them to be further corrupted by the dealers who flocked to our part of town. When we finally accepted the reality that the heroin "youth-quake" was upon us, we reluctantly adjusted our admission policy to reflect this disturbing trend.

6

Starting Treatment

Those treatment candidates who successfully passed through the rigorous intake process then met with the staff physician in order to be "medically cleared" to ingest methadone. Candidates told the doctor how much heroin they had been consuming on a daily basis. The medical staff used this information to determine how many milligrams of methadone to prescribe for the clients. Many clients started at around 30 milligrams a day and had their dosage increased as needed. The physicians at our facility were reluctant to give clients more than 100 milligrams per day, but this is not the case at every methadone clinic. I was told that at some clinics, clients are allowed to consume upwards of 150 milligrams of methadone a day.

It was never clear at the outset exactly how much methadone a person would require, though factors like body weight and estimated metabolic rate could sometimes serve as guideposts for the doctor. Some clients stabilized on 30 or 50 milligrams, dosages that are considered to be on the lower side, while others required 100 milligrams a day just to feel like something approaching normal. When a client's methadone dose is too low, he continues using heroin occasionally in order to maintain the level of opiates in his system. This is known as "chipping." Some of our clients, for example, felt just fine on 40 milligrams, but they wanted to feel more than fine. They wanted to feel high, so they continually asked the doctors to increase their dosage.

This raises an interesting question: do clients get high from methadone? The answer depends on whom you ask. Many clients confessed to getting a slight buzz for the first twenty minutes or so after drinking their doses (especially if they had per-suaded the doctor to increase their dosage beyond what they really needed). Others stated that they had completely lost the ability to feel high from any drug, including methadone, and that they used methadone to "get straight," rather than to get high. These clients did not feel ready to face the world without their daily dose of methadone. However, if a non-opiate-addicted individual were to drink even a small dose of methadone, he would probably feel extremely intoxicated and woozy for a very long time, which illustrates just how potent a narcotic substance methadone is.

Just as some of our clients persuaded the clinic physicians to give them more methadone than they actually needed, other clients deliberately kept their doses too low. They did this be-cause they still wanted to abuse heroin (and feel high in the process). But when clients have enough methadone in their sys-tem—and what constitutes "enough" varies from person to per-son—the methadone blocks the heroin from getting through to their brain cells, preventing them from feeling high. For obvious reasons, this is known as a "blocking dose."

As I have already noted, heroin addiction assaults its vic-tims psychologically and physically. It is the physical depen-dence that must be tackled first. If, for example, a heroin addict uses twenty bags intravenously per day, but one day cannot get any heroin, that single day of involuntary abstinence can cause the opiate addict to feel any or all of the following agonizing symptoms of opiate withdrawal: severe nausea, gut-wrenching diarrhea, brutal migraine headaches, muscle cramping and pain (especially in the legs), excessive perspiration, insomnia, depres-sion, joint pain, and relentless fatigue.

People on methadone therefore need to take their doses on a daily basis. Otherwise, they will suffer all of the terrible symp-toms of heroin withdrawal. Indeed, many of our clients likened their methadone treatment to being restrained by a pair of "liq-uid handcuffs." They literally could not make a move without considering how they were going to get themselves to the clinic each and every day of their lives. On a positive note, those cli-ents who took their methadone exactly as prescribed and man-aged to avoid all illicit drug use, eventually stopped physically craving heroin.

Some clients became so fixated on their methadone doses that they came to believe that the nurses were "skimming a little off the top." While this practice is not totally unheard of, I do not believe that it was taking place at our clinic. Nevertheless, these clients, who may have been suffering from at least some of the symptoms associated with obsessive compulsive disorder, speculated endlessly about how much powdery sediment should remain at the bottom of their cups in order for them to be absolutely certain that they had not been cheated on their methadone dose. If, on any given day, there was less residue in their empty cups than usual, they suspected the dosing nurse of "skimming," or giving them a lower dose than had been prescribed for them.

Ours was a "blind-dosing" clinic, which means that we were asked not to tell our clients the exact amount of methadone they were ingesting. In theory, blind-dosing is supposed to help clients focus less on their precise dosage, and more on their problems with addiction. In practice, however, the opposite appeared to be true. Blind-dosing seemed to cause many of our clients to focus obsessively on how much methadone they were receiving.

From a medical vantage point, starting on a methadone maintenance program is very serious business, and the side effects of methadone consumption are not at all pleasant. For instance, many of our clients gained weight, which they under-standably found distressing. It was possible that the methadone was causing them to get heavier. On the other hand, for the first time in years they were eating three square meals a day, rather than grabbing snacks on the run. This significant behavioral shift may have also contributed to their weight gain. Many clients also complained of worsening dental health and tooth loss, problems they attributed exclusively to methadone. When I asked the nurses about this, they said it was hard to determine whether the methadone was causing the tooth decay, or whether our clients were just suffering from the effects of a lifetime's worth of dental neglect. In addition, some of our clients complained about brutal constipation, while others claimed that methadone had turned them into insomniacs. Finally, when our clients did not have enough methadone in their systems, they often experienced excruciating pain in their leg muscles.

The clinic offered two different dosing times: 9:00-12:00 in the morning and 4:00-6:00 in the afternoon. Clients could dose only during designated half-hour periods (say from 4:30-5:00

p.m.). People who were caring for small children or working at full-time jobs were given priority for the much-coveted morning dosing slots. In reality, however, neither of the two dosing times was convenient for those clients who worked standard business hours. In fact, the few clients who worked from 9:00 to 5:00 were in a continuous state of anxiety. They constantly had to come up with new excuses to get to the clinic during the day without telling their bosses where they were really going. In addition to the aforementioned lack of insurance coverage for methadone treatment, dose scheduling was yet another impediment that discouraged many of our clients from joining the mainstream world of 9:00-5:00 workaday life.

Generally speaking, our clients preferred to dose in the morning because it made them feel better for the rest of the day. Those who were obliged to dose in the late afternoon often complained about nighttime sleeplessness and daytime withdrawal symptoms. More and more of the clients were being required to dose in the afternoons, because the morning dosing hours had become overcrowded. Right before I resigned, the "afternoon clients" were requesting the total dissolution of the afternoon dosing slot. I could hardly blame them for making the request, because I knew how much healthier they felt when they dosed in the morning.

The rather rigorous conditions and requirements of treatment included the following: engage in no illegal behavior; abstain from all illicit drug use; attend a series of orientation lectures; participate in individual counseling and group counseling (both on a weekly basis); provide supervised urine samples—also on a weekly basis—for off-site laboratory urinalysis; obtain a primary care physician; have regular, documented physical examinations; and take part in educational seminars.

The clients' urine samples were tested each week for the presence of heroin, cocaine, marijuana, alcohol, and benzodiazapines (or "benzos," for short), of which Xanax® and Klonopin® are two prime examples. The clinic was willing to pay for these various lab tests, because many of the clients were able to abstain from heroin thanks to the methadone. But they often had more difficulty staying away from other drugs, particularly benzos, which are anti-anxiety pills. In fact, some of our clients struggled enormously with benzos, which are highly addictive and have a synergistic effect when taken along with methadone. In combination, the two drugs can cause a person to feel extremely high. Unfortunately, some methadone clients make money by selling benzos to their peers. At our clinic, those who were caught illicitly using or selling benzos or any other illegal drugs were promptly disciplined by the clinic's administration.

In addition, any clients who were deemed to be "out of compliance" with any of the treatment requirements were penalized. Some non-compliant clients were placed on probation; others were "involuntarily detoxified" from methadone. Punishment depended on the nature of the infraction. When it was decided that non-compliant clients had to be involuntarily detoxified, they were generally "weaned off" methadone at the accelerated pace of thirty or sixty days.

Consider for a moment that a comfortable, "tapered" methadone detoxification involves lowering the dosage by 2.5 milligrams per month. If clients who are dosing at a rate of 80 milligrams a day are administratively detoxified, this means that they have to reduce to 0 milligrams a day in just one or two months' time. Toward the end of the month, the withdrawal symptoms will make them feel extraordinarily uncomfortable, which suggests exactly how harsh a punishment involuntary detoxification is. Clients always had the right to "appeal" by pleading their cases to the director. Unfortunately, most of our clients feared all authority figures and dreaded the idea of appealing and so avoided it at all costs.

In keeping with this "carrot-and-stick" model of administering punishments and rewards, those clients who were fully compliant with all of the treatment requirements could eventually earn "take-home" doses. As the name says, a "take-home" dose is a little bottled dose that can be refrigerated and consumed in the comfort and privacy of one's own home. At our clinic, the most compliant clients could earn up to four take-home methadone doses per week. However, if a client who had earned the maximum four take-homes committed a single treatment infraction, then all four take-home doses could be abruptly revoked.

The Benefits of Methadone Treatment

Working in a methadone clinic can be very trying at times, but there is no doubt about the fact that methadone treatment saves lives. When clients utilize treatment properly, the results can be impressive indeed. Several clients on my own caseload had managed to turn their lives around completely. And every one of them attributed that success to their methadone treatment.

These clients had stopped using drugs completely, and consequently, they had also stopped breaking the law. In other words, because they no longer needed to raise large quantities of cash in a short amount of time to support their drug habits, they no longer needed to rob, deal, shoplift, or prostitute. Beyond this, some of them had found jobs. And their overall level of functioning, both at work and at home, had increased dramatically.

Some of my clients had reached all of these goals in a matter of months, which, I believe, is nothing short of miraculous. Even more significantly, they had lifted themselves out of hopelessness and inertia by creating their own miracles. The gratification and pride they felt as a result of having achieved all of these important goals is difficult to describe in words. Some of my most successful clients cried tears of joy and relief during our counseling sessions. It was almost impossible for them to believe how far they had come.

As a result of all their hard work, their self-esteem increased enormously, and we counselors could see the changes in their body language, their posture, and their facial expressions. It was wonderful to see men and women who had previously neglected their appearance suddenly taking pride in how they looked, dressed, and presented themselves to the world. For instance, it was always a very good sign when a female client who had previously worked as a prostitute started to dress more modestly.

Naturally, we counselors felt a tremendous sense of satisfaction when our clients did well. To be sure, the clients had done all the hard work of getting drug-free and staying drug-free, but we staffers had the pleasure of knowing that we had helped them reach that point. Our successful clients also tended to express their gratitude to us quite frequently, which only added to our sense of accomplishment as their counselors. Whenever one of my clients made this kind of dramatic turnaround, I felt extremely proud and happy, and I was reminded of why I had become a counselor in the first place. I do not know if it is even possible to get such deeply satisfying emotional rewards outside of the counseling field.

Many of our clients had been "written off" as lost causes by their family members, the police, and their probation officers, so it was especially gratifying for them to prove all of the naysayers in their lives wrong. In addition to reducing their drug use and criminal activity, while at the same time significantly increasing their employability and self-esteem, methadone treatment had provided these clients with a much-needed sense of community.

Many of our clients had been shy, lonely, extremely isolated and introverted individuals who had become even more reclusive and alone as a result of their extensive drug use. After all, isolation is one of the main features of addiction. For drug addicts, the danger of solitude and feeling lonely all of the time is that the temptation to keep using drugs, in order to combat or forget their loneliness, can become overpowering.

Before earning their "take-home" doses, methadone clients are required to report to the clinic every single day. This regimen gives their days a sense of structure and purpose. It also compels them to socialize with others, rather than withdraw from society or isolate themselves. Over time, many methadone clients come to view themselves and their comrades in treatment as a community of recovering addicts, and they start to feel as if "We're in this together now." The more compliant and motivated clients develop a strong sense of connection and loyalty to the other clients, to some of the staff members, and even to the clinic itself. Moreover, they begin to feel concerned about the physical and emotional well-being of their fellow clients. Among other things, it's this newfound concern for others that helps them to break out of their isolation and become re-engaged not only in their own lives, but also in the lives of their loved ones.

Clients who utilize methadone treatment properly also experience significant improvements in their mental and physical health. Because they have stopped using drugs, they no longer run the risk of developing abscesses, collapsed veins, or other medical problems. They have also eliminated their chances of overdosing or being poisoned by whatever substance the heroin may have been cut with—rat poison, bleach, and the like. Furthermore, they have radically lowered their chances of contracting HIV or the various strains of hepatitis.

Highly motivated clients also tend to see their doctors with greater regularity. This enables them to get medical attention for their chronic health issues and to start practicing preventive care so as to avoid developing new health problems. Drug-free clients who are HIV-positive also tend to be more compliant about taking their HIV medications. Finally, compliant clients tend to have much healthier sleeping and eating patterns than their non-compliant peers.

There are still more benefits for compliant methadone clients. Not only do they begin to address their physical health problems, but they also start to address their mental health issues. Because they are no longer in a drug-induced fog, they have a renewed sense of clarity that can be both frightening and exhilarating. If they have an underlying depressive or anxiety disorder, they can finally begin to use therapy and the appropriate psychopharmaceutical medications rather than street drugs to ameliorate the problem. All of these improvements give compliant methadone clients peace of mind and a higher quality of life.

While it is true that all clients have to contend with the dealers who like to hover around methadone clinics, they also come face-to-face with wonderful role models on a daily basis. Every methadone therapy group contains a mixture of clients who are drug-free and clients who are still struggling. This means that every time struggling clients attend a group therapy session, they are exposed to individuals who are doing extremely well in treatment. This can inspire the struggling clients to believe that they, too, can become motivated to overcome inertia in order to become clean and sober. Just as a beginning tennis player can benefit from playing against a more experienced tennis player, addicts who are still actively battling their addictions can benefit enormously from working with clients who are drug-free.

Some clients do so well in methadone treatment that they eventually taper off completely and leave. One evening, I had the distinct privilege of hearing such a former client give a talk to a group of clients and counselors. Adam had called Susan, the clinic director, to let her know that he was still clean and sober after leaving treatment three years earlier. He wanted to express his gratitude to the clinic staff, and had been racking his brains for several months about the best way to say thanks. He had finally decided to offer his services as a motivational speaker.

A shy man, Adam said that he had hesitated to call for a few weeks, as he dreaded public speaking. In the end, he had decided that it was too important for him to share his story, and he would not let his shyness stop him. I only wish that more clients had attended his presentation. His words were moving and truly inspiring.

He had been in treatment for a total of six years. During the first two years, by his own admission, he had spent a fair amount of time trying to deceive his counselor and "get over on" the urinalysis system. In retrospect, he regretted wasting so much time, but he also saw those first two years of treatment as something he "had to go through in order to get to the other side."

He explained: "After a certain point, I just lost interest in the drug scene, and I also got fed up with myself for what I had done to my family." In his drug-abusing days, nearly all of his relatives had stopped speaking to him. "But they never lost all faith in me, and I'm so grateful for that," he added. "They were just waiting for me to come around, and they believed that some day I would. I'm sure their faith in me helped me to get clean."

Once Adam had been drug-free in the clinic's treatment program for two years, he felt secure enough about his recovery to begin tapering off his methadone dosage, which he did over the course of another two years. After he left the clinic, at first he felt a little shaky about maintaining his sobriety. Nevertheless, he stayed clean. Over time, he proved to himself and his family members that he could stay sober, even without methadone.

During his drug-abusing days, Adam never would have dreamed of borrowing a significant sum of money from a family member. They would have said no and he could not have blamed them for it. Now, however, he had changed his life so radically that one of his relatives offered to lend him the money he needed to start a small business, which he promptly did. The business had done so well that he was able to pay back the loan in full, and of all his post-treatment accomplishments, this one filled him with the most pride.

"Your family lent you money?" one audience member asked incredulously.

"I couldn't believe it either. After all the times I'd stolen from my family, they still loved me. I guess they had forgiven me, too."

"You sound like you have an amazing family. I don't think my family will ever forgive me like your family forgave you," said another audience member.

"That's what I thought," Adam responded. "I thought I'd burned all my bridges years earlier, and that they would never, ever trust me again. And I have to tell you that it took them a while to trust me again. I guess I needed to prove myself to them."

A third audience member asked: "Be honest. When they lent you that money, weren't you a little tempted to blow it all on drugs?"

"It's funny. I thought I might be. And I guess I was tempted for a split second. But then it passed. The craving came and went. And right afterward, I had this thought: 'My family trusts me again, and there's no way in hell that I'm going to screw this up.' Looking back on it now, I think that was a very important moment in my recovery, because money used to be the biggest trigger for me. But now money didn't have the same power over me that it once had. I think that was the moment I'd been praying for all those years."

Then Joan, one of the counselors, said: "Your story is very inspiring, but what would you say to people who are still struggling with drug cravings? You've gone through this incredibly difficult journey, and you've survived, and even thrived. But what would you say to folks who are worried that they 'don't have what it takes' to make the same journey that you've made?"

"Let me tell you, when I was still messing with drugs during those first two years at the clinic, I would look at the sober people in my treatment group, and I would think: 'I'm nothing like them. I just don't have what it takes to get clean. I might as well give up.' I really thought they were from another planet. But later on—much later on—I realized this was just an excuse. The only difference between the sober people in my group and myself at the time was that they had committed themselves to their recovery and I hadn't. That was truly the only difference between us. When I finally committed myself to my own sobriety, I saw that I could do it, too. And if I can do it, anyone can. It doesn't take special powers. There's nothing magical about it. You just have to be persistent. And you can never forget. One day at a time, right?"

"What do you mean, you can never forget?" someone else asked.

"I can never forget just how bad things got, because they got pretty bad. I hated myself. My family had stopped taking my calls. I can never forget how badly I treated the people I loved the most, or the way I stopped caring about everything."

"You seem very grateful," said Ben, another counselor.

"I am. I count my blessings every day. Not everyone gets a second chance in life, but that's what I've been given. And I'm not going to blow it. I'm going to run my business, and travel, and start a family, and do everything I ever dreamed of doing."

When he finished speaking, several audience members wiped tears from their eyes. Adam was also overcome by emotion. Before leaving, he shook hands with Susan, the director, and thanked her for giving him the opportunity to share his story.

Clearly, the benefits of methadone treatment for highly motivated individuals are indisputable. As our clients often said, "If you work the program, the program works for you." While it's true that some of our clients had turned their lives around completely in methadone treatment, too many of our other clients continued to struggle unsuccessfully against their emotional and psychological urges to use heroin and other drugs. Therefore, the greatest challenge for treatment providers remains figuring out how to equip all of our clients—not only the most motivated among them—with the coping skills that will enable them to fight off their most intense drug cravings "one day at a time" for the rest of their lives.

8

The Self-Medicating Theory

As long as there is pain and suffering in the world, people will want to escape from it by whatever means necessary, which is why the problem of heroin addiction (and addiction in general) will probably never go away completely. According to Edward Khantzian, the renowned Harvard-affiliated scholar who developed the "self-medicating" theory, addicts tend to be individuals who have been deeply wounded psychologically, emotionally, spiritually, or physically, and who in turn "self-medicate" or anesthetize themselves by abusing alcohol and/or drugs.

Many of the clients at the clinic self-medicated to combat the overwhelming symptoms of severe mental illness, such as hearing voices or seeing visions. Others were plagued by recurring nightmares about childhood abuse, and they had discovered that heroin enabled them to sleep without dreaming. Still others had been taunted incessantly during their school days for being illiterate or learning disabled, and so they had eventually turned to drugs to quell their painful feelings of humiliation, shame, and despair.

Beyond this, a significant number of them self-medicated to numb the pain caused by back problems, arthritis, and other chronic, debilitating physical conditions. At some point in their lives, they had been prescribed opiate painkillers such as codeine, but their doctors had eventually weaned them off their prescription opiates, hoping to prevent them from developing long-term pill habits. Unfortunately, rather than switching to non-pharmaceutical methods of pain management (as their doctors had suggested), they had merely exchanged their pill habits for heroin habits. In many cases, they made this switch because heroin is considerably cheaper and easier to come by on the streets than prescription pills, yet it is just as effective for stopping pain, if not more so.

The rule I was taught at the clinic is that depressive people often self-medicate with cocaine, an upper that temporarily lifts their spirits, and that angry people often self-medicate with heroin, a downer that briefly dampens their feelings of rage. That said, there are numerous exceptions to this rule. In other words, my colleagues and I worked with a significant number of angry cocaine addicts and just as many depressed heroin addicts.

Because of their unique brain chemistry, many bipolar clients seem to be particularly fond of cocaine. Not only do they use cocaine during depressive periods, as one would expect, but also during floridly manic phases. During a bout of mania, cocaine, paradoxically, appears to induce a soothing effect in bipolar individuals, calming them down instead of revving them up further. In addition, the psychiatrist who served as our staff consultant explained that some people with attention deficit hyperactivity disorder (ADHD) appear to be susceptible to developing problems with substance abuse. He also said that they tend to gravitate toward cocaine and nicotine, since the stimulating effects of these drugs help them focus and concentrate, if only in short bursts.

Incidentally, it was my observation that clients of all personality types were fond of smoking marijuana. Some favored marijuana for its strong analgesic properties; others simply enjoyed a marijuana high almost as much as a heroin "nod." Quite a few of them liked it so much that they had managed to kick all drugs except marijuana.

Khantzian has uncovered a considerable amount of empirical evidence to support his self-medicating theory. Quite understandably, many of the clients were profoundly comforted by the idea of a scientific explanation for their condition. Unfortunately, a number of them found ways to turn this explanation into an excuse for continuing to abuse drugs. Simply put, instead of making every effort to stop self-medicating, they used the theory as a means of rationalizing their continued drug use, claiming: "I'm sick. Leave me alone to 'self-medicate' my pain.

Don't you see? I'm not responsible for my behavior. I can't help myself."

Whenever I was with a methadone client who was content to make excuses rather than changes, I was reminded of the wise words of one of my social work teachers. He used to say that clients feel deeply gratified—and justifiably so—when they first acquire some fresh insight into their self-destructive tendencies. But that is only the beginning. Until they act on their newfound insight by making some definitive changes in their behavior, they cannot be considered fully engaged in treatment.

9

Triggers

Heroin is as seductive as a siren beckoning from the jagged rocks—and just as dangerous. Once our clients were no longer experiencing the physical urges to use heroin, they still had to combat their psychological and emotional urges, which can be far more difficult to conquer. In our counseling sessions, I encouraged my clients to identify all of their "triggers," which are the environmental cues that continue to cause opiate addicts to crave heroin and other drugs, even after they have stabilized physically on methadone.

A trigger can be any "person, place, or thing" that makes a client want to use heroin. And a "triggering effect" can be so powerful that it can actually set off a chain reaction of physical responses, such as excessive sweating, a mouth-watering sensation, hot and cold flashes, and a bitter taste in the back of the throat.

My more seasoned colleagues explained to me that a trigger can take the form of a spouse who also abuses drugs, or a favorite meeting place, or certain emotional states, such as boredom, or loneliness, or stress. Being involved in the "drug scene" and associating only with other drug addicts are obvious triggers. Having too much cash or too much free time can also be treacherous for a heroin addict. The truth of the matter is that almost all methadone clients—even the most stable among them—can be powerfully triggered by the mere sight of fellow clients whose pinpoint pupils and nodding heads indicate that they are high on heroin. Some of our clients even named vomiting as a trigger, because throwing up is what a lot of people do right after they shoot up and right before oblivion sets in. Consequently, some heroin addicts develop an almost sentimental attachment to the physical sensation of nausea.

Not all triggers make sense to non-addicts. But for addicts, they are inescapable. Identifying their triggers was generally an easy counseling exercise for most of our clients. They could usually rattle off a couple of dozen or so triggers in less than five minutes. It was finding ways to avoid their triggers that proved to be far more difficult. Indeed, for many of the clients I treated, learning how to avoid triggers was the hardest task they had to accomplish during the entire course of their treatment.

Suppose, for example, that an addict's wife is his primary drug-using companion, and that she has no interest in quitting, but that he feels ready to quit. Obviously, it is very difficult to abstain from drug use if your significant other is not abstaining along with you. If this man is serious about "going straight," but his wife is not, he may soon find himself contemplating separation. Thus the stakes can be enormous for the heroin addict who is seeking sobriety.

I never suggested to clients that they consider leaving their partners in order to get clean. It would have been unethical and inappropriate for me to do so. Rather, I asked open-ended questions until my clients reached their own conclusions about what steps to take next. Sometimes during that process, clients came to the realization that they might have to go to great lengths, not only to get clean and sober, but also to stay alive. Some of them were prepared to make major sacrifices for the sake of their sobriety, while others were not ready or willing to take such radical steps.

Regarding client marriages, we occasionally treated couples at the clinic, but it was nearly always disastrous when we did. Invariably, when one partner was doing well, the other partner was not, and the faltering one dragged the other down. Without exception, this happened to every couple I observed at the clinic.

Considering that it takes superhuman strength for an addict with a sober spouse to get clean, imagine how difficult it is when both partners are struggling with addiction. Husbands and wives were always assigned to different counselors at our clinic, but even this was not enough of a preventive measure. I would contend that most opiate-addicted couples require completely separate treatment at different clinics.

A similar problem arose when clients met and started dating each other while in treatment. In most of these cases, neither client was particularly stable to begin with, and getting together did not improve their chances of recovery. HIV was another issue that sometimes came up when clients began dating each other. By law, every individual's HIV-status is a confidential matter; under no circumstances can a counselor ever discuss one person's HIV-status with another. This meant that if an HIV-positive client began dating an HIV-negative client—and we staffers were aware of the HIV-status of both clients—we were strictly prohibited from revealing anything to either person. All we could do was stress to both individuals the importance of practicing safe sex at all times, as well as the importance of communicating openly and honestly with one's partner. Beyond that, we could only hope that the HIV-positive client would be honest with his or her partner and that the couple would, in fact, practice safe sex on a consistent basis.

Even platonic friendships suffered at the clinic. I saw more client friendships fall into ruins than I ever thought humanly possible. One friend would accuse the other of stealing money, or ruining a drug deal, or neglecting his or her children. Then there would be a terrible fight. In the end, the friendship would be over almost as quickly as it had begun. Because many of the clients had never experienced anything resembling a healthy human relationship, they had considerable difficulty establishing genuine, agenda-free connections with other people. On top of everything else, it seemed that drugs had robbed them of their capacity to forge happy romances and healthy friendships.

What I tried to bear in mind as I observed all of these clinic friendships and romances imploding, is that each of us can manage only incremental—not monumental—change. Thus an immense supply of patience was required of both methadone clients and their counselors. I noticed that our clients tended to be much harder on themselves than their counselors were. I also found that it was especially important for clients to forgive themselves when they first realized that methadone was not going to be the panacea they had hoped it would be. Only very rarely was a client able to stop using all illicit drugs immediately upon entering treatment. Many clients took months or even years to shake all their bad habits.

As I have mentioned, methadone cannot be considered a cure-all, because it assuages physical urges only, while doing nothing to curb emotional cravings. The only way our clients could permanently vanquish their emotional urges was to determine in their counseling sessions precisely which triggers they were willing to jettison in order to achieve lasting sobriety. In essence, addicts have to want recovery more than anything they have ever wanted before, a tall order considering that the elimination of triggers often requires bidding adieu to old friends and lovers.

I regret to say that for many of our clients, the clinic itself constituted an enormous trigger. When they saw other clients walking around high, they were powerfully reminded of just how easy it could be to forget their own troubles. It did not help matters that some clients were selling illicit drugs to other clients. It takes extraordinary strength for addicts to "just say no" when someone is waving drugs right in front of them. In addition, dealers who were not our clients flocked to the area, like moths to a flame. There also seemed to be a tangled web of complicated connections among clients who had known one another from the past, and the staff had little or no understanding of the true nature of most of these dangerous liaisons.

A typical conversation about triggers between a counselor and a client might go something like this:

"It's easy for you counselors to tell us to change our lives all around, but it's not that easy for us. Would you want to ditch all your old friends and stop going to all of your old hangouts?"

"I understand that it's not easy."

"You're damn right it's not. What am I supposed to do? Where am I supposed to go?"

"You could go to a self-help meeting. That's always a good place to start. You might meet some new friends there who are trying to stay clean, just like you."

"I know, but right afterward I still have to go back to my neighborhood, and my dealer lives right around the corner from my apartment."

"Have you considered moving? It sounds like your neighborhood is a pretty powerful trigger for you."

"I can't move right now. It's too expensive. I can't come up with first and last months' rent, plus a security deposit."

"You still seem to have enough money to buy drugs. Your last several urine screens have tested positive."

"That's different."

"I don't see how it's different, but you know how the program works: if the dirty urine screens don't stop, you'll be placed on probation. Perhaps it's time to consider going into a residential treatment program for a while. I'd be happy to call for an application, or better yet, we could make the call together."

"Look. I'm just not ready to do that right now."

"Okay. If you don't feel prepared to move or to consider residential treatment, let's think of some other steps you can take to reduce the triggering effects of your neighborhood. You could start by throwing away your dealer's phone number and beeper number."

"Are you kidding? I've got those numbers memorized! I think they're tattooed on my brain."

"Well, we have to do something about all these triggers."

"You really don't get it, do you? It doesn't matter where I live, or how I spend my time. A dollar bill can trigger me. The color of a stop sign can remind me of the color of the lighter I use to cook my dope. Don't you see? I'm surrounded by triggers, and I know I always will be. Every time I turn around, there's another one."

What's so typical about this hypothetical counselor-client discussion of triggers is its circular nature. The counselor threw out a series of suggestions, and the client came up with excuse after excuse to reject every last one of them. This imaginary conversation suggests how daunting it can be for clients to change their lives and achieve lasting sobriety. It also indicates how challenging it can be for counselors to work with clients who are still what we refer to in the field as "resistant," or reluctant to make all of the lifestyle changes necessary for them to get clean.

At one point, the local press in our area identified a particularly potent batch of heroin as the cause of four deaths across the state. Oddly enough, the newspaper articles about these deaths had a very potent "triggering effect" on some of our clients, who said that they desperately wanted to get their hands on the "killer dope" (as it had been dubbed by journalists). What was hard for me to understand initially was that in their hunt for this "killer dope," these clients were actually not expressing suicidal tendencies. Rather, they were only striving—as usual—to recapture the euphoric rush of their very first heroin high. Because I was still a novice clinician, I had momentarily forgotten that for active opiate addicts, the search for the Ultimate High is actually comparable to the legendary medieval knights' quest for the Holy Grail.

10

The Needle

For many addicts, the needle itself takes on a sort of mystical power. Movies with drug scenes, particularly the ritual where the heroin is "cooked" and prepared for use, illustrate this principle perfectly. Consider for a moment the various tools that comprise an addict's paraphernalia, or his "works." There is the spoon, the tourniquet, the flame, the powder melting hypnotically into liquid, the liquid sliding first into the syringe, and then through the needle into the vein.

For an addict, the sight of someone getting high on a movie screen can be more erotically charged than the sexiest of seduction scenes. Of course, what you will also notice about every celluloid drug-using sequence is that the needle itself always takes center stage. The fact is that, with certain heroin addicts, their powerful emotional attachment to the needle eventually grows stronger over time than their addiction to the heroin itself. As their ticket to blissful oblivion, the needle becomes fetishized, transformed into an object of worship and desire.

Not every client at the clinic used drugs intravenously (even though they had always been told that the needle high is the most intense kind of high). Many clients who snorted or smoked heroin could not bring themselves to cross that invisible line into the world of intravenous drug use. As long as they only used heroin nasally, they could go on telling themselves that they were not "hardcore junkies." Their rationalization was that only an addict who actually injects heroin is compelled to carry the burden of that cruel stigma.

Those who had crossed the threshold into the world of intravenous drug use often discussed the use of needles with their counselors. They hated to be stigmatized by mainstream society as "no-good junkies." But as much as they resented the stigma, they implicitly understood that as far as the "straight" world was concerned, they had taken a leap into the darkness from which they could never fully return. Maybe it is the sight of blood or the thought of breaking the skin, but whatever the reason, intravenous drug use is taboo and deeply frowned upon in most sectors of mainstream society.

The I.V. heroin users at the clinic also talked about the hypocrisy and double standards of the so-called "straight" world. They pointed out, for instance, that during the seventies and eighties, it was actually considered "cool" to snort a few lines of cocaine at a party. However, if any of them had ever dared to shoot heroin at one of those same parties, the other guests would have been disgusted at the sight.

For some individuals with a needle obsession, merely looking at a syringe can trigger the beginnings of an intense high. Others do not feel high simply from gazing at a needle, but their mouths start to water, and they get a very strange, almost metallic taste in the back of their mouths. They start to sweat profusely in anticipation of getting high any minute. Some addicts with needle fixations will inject whatever is around—alcohol, or even tap water—just to experience the physical sensation of injecting something into their flesh. This compulsive injecting can sometimes develop into a separate, equally dangerous habit in its own right. Some of our clients reported that when they had first started using heroin, they never could have conceived of using needles. Then they had ended up not only using needles, but shooting the drugs directly into the veins in their necks.

I once spoke with a male heroin addict who said: "I have a love/hate relationship with needles. I have days when I feel like most 'straight' people feel about needles. They totally gross me out. But then I have other days when I feel like there's nothing cooler than shooting up. And women really like it."

"Do they?" I asked.

"Well, obviously not all women. But some do. The same ones who like bikers and rebel-outlaw types like guys who use needles. They think it's macho or something."

"Really?"

"I guess so. Some girls want guys who 'live on the edge,' and needles can be a part of that. But the messed-up thing is that after a while, the needle takes over your life, and then it stops being sexy. In fact, you stop caring about sex at all."

The irony was not lost on him.

My clients informed me that people with intense needle addictions can shoot up dozens of times a day. This can cause abscesses, infections, and the collapsing of veins, among other problems. It can take an hour or longer for an addict with too many collapsed veins to find a usable one. And when all of an addict's veins collapse—even the ones in his neck—he is forced to shoot drugs directly into his muscles (often the muscles in his upper arm or thighs). This intra-muscular use can lead to the formation of other painful, festering abscesses. Also, needle users are more prone than other addicts to developing an excruciating condition called "cotton fever," the symptoms of which include clammy skin, projectile vomiting, and a high fever.

Heroin addicts with needle fixations are similar to drug addicts who get a genuinely bigger rush from the shoplifting or prostituting they do to support their habit than they do from actually using the drug. In the substance abuse counseling field, this phenomenon is known as the formation of a "substitute addiction," whereby an addict literally replaces one addiction with another. According to some of my veteran colleagues, there are times when such a substitution may be a sort of "lateral move" that some addicts make when they are seriously contemplating going straight, but are still not quite ready to commit themselves fully to the task. Unfortunately, however, even if substituting one addiction for another can sometimes indicate the beginning of a shift in the right direction, it can also be extremely dangerous.

For instance, those of our clients who enjoyed shoplifting asserted that it was the ultimate way to "get over on The Man." They also said that they experienced an almost sexual thrill from the risk of getting caught by store security or the police. For those who became addicted to sex instead, picking up strangers in bars and night clubs became their "substitute" addiction. These clients insisted to their counselors that engaging in anonymous but "safe" sex was less dangerous than abusing drugs. In reality, of course, abusing drugs and engaging in indiscriminate sex with total strangers are both equally hazardous games of Russian Roulette.

11

Prostitution

It is expensive to use heroin and other drugs, especially when you consider that addicts continually have to increase the amount of heroin they are using just to feel normal (that is, not "sick as a dog"). This harsh reality often causes heroin addicts to engage in all sorts of dangerous, criminal, and sometimes even violent behavior in order to obtain drugs. It is precisely this kind of behavior that stigmatizes opiate addicts and makes so many people despise and fear them. Criminality further strips addicts of their already depleted supplies of self-respect, and this, in turn, adds to the emotional numbness that the drugs themselves induce in them.

Many of the female clients I worked with had been reduced to selling their bodies for drugs at some point in their lives. (I was surprised to learn that none of my male clients had ever worked as prostitutes. Or if they had, they never acknowledged it in counseling.) It is one thing, many of my female clients said, to sell all your belongings for drugs, but it is an indignity of a far higher order to be forced to sell your own flesh.

Those relatively few women at the clinic who had been lucky enough to avoid prostitution were understandably proud of the fact. Somehow, they had always been able to scrape together enough cash in other ways, and they had never taken that final perilous step down the road to total self-destruction. In a disturbing power game of "one-upmanship," some of the women who had not prostituted themselves held this over the heads of the ones who had. Often they went straight for the jugular, saying, "Well, I may have sold everything I ever owned, but at least I never stooped as low as you did. I never sold my own body." Some individuals who despise themselves belittle others in a bitter effort to boost their own faltering sense of self-worth.

Clients who had resorted to prostitution at one point or another had worked hard to hang onto their self-respect by setting some strict guidelines for themselves. For example (just like in the movies), most of them made it a rule never to kiss their johns or "dates," as a lot of them called their customers. They preferred to reserve that one small but precious bit of intimacy for their real-life lovers.

Not surprisingly, most of these women had a great deal of difficulty sustaining long-term relationships. Some said that drugs "satisfied" all of their hungers, including their appetites for food and sex. They admitted that they had trouble with intimacy, in part because they did not know how to achieve it, but also because (by their own admission) they tended to put their drugs before their partners.

Unfortunately, not all of the women practiced safe sex. If their "dates" offered to pay double for unprotected sex, many of them acquiesced. This was tragic, not only for the women, but for their customers as well. All of them were placing themselves at risk for a wide variety of sexually transmitted diseases.

Some of them worked for escort services, or at strip clubs, or as "dominatrixes." And, of course, many of the women worked for pimps, who terrorized them and beat them up frequently, and also demanded most of their earnings.

Many of them stated that they worked the "lunch shift," which involved standing on designated street corners throughout the city at the noon hour. Men would drive by, look directly into their eyes, pull over, and arrange to meet them somewhere. Even though the women did not dress as provocatively during the "lunch shift" as they did at night, they said that the men could still tell the prostitutes from the other female pedestrians because of the prolonged eye contact that the prostitutes made with their potential customers.

Many of these women had started prostituting only after they had already started using heroin. A few of them, however, had started prostituting before using the drug. Some had been introduced to heroin by their "dates" or their pimps. Up to that point, they had dabbled in other drugs, such as cocaine and marijuana, but once they tried heroin, they became enslaved to prostitution. They could not stomach the thought of "turning tricks" unless they were totally high, and they needed to turn tricks in order to get money for drugs. Consequently, their lives had quickly disintegrated into a vicious cycle of buying drugs, getting high, working the streets to earn cash for drugs, and then going out to buy drugs all over again. A number of these women characterized their own behavior as reminiscent of a hamster running on an exercise wheel: there is a great deal of frantic movement, but no forward motion.

Those who had occasionally serviced customers while sober inevitably felt dirty and degraded immediately thereafter. When they were high, they said they could almost pretend that they were having an "out-of-body" experience, or that the whole sordid experience was happening to some other woman. Their physical selves were being violated, but their souls were miles away (or so they tried to tell themselves). Most of them understood that the heroin was what enabled them to keep their feelings at bay.

Some of them had never experienced a single loving sexual relationship. Also, their only friendships—or what they called "drugships"—were with untrustworthy people they had met in the drug world. They had come to believe that real love was something that only happened in books and movies—never in real life. Our female clients taught me that if a woman is deprived of love for long enough, she may eventually surrender to despair and turn her own body into a commodity.

Some clients who were still prostituting said they were addicted to the easy money that the job could sometimes generate. It would have been tough, they felt, to settle for a job that paid minimum wage after earning the kind of money they were accustomed to earning from prostitution. Also, many of them said they lacked the necessary confidence and patience to return to school or look for conventional work. Quite frankly, some of them were totally uninterested in the idea of working in the mainstream world. They said they found most straight people square and boring. And after prostituting for so many years, they could barely imagine doing anything else.

Despite their "tough-gal" facades, however, they sometimes acknowledged that prostitution had taken them on a much more painful journey than they could ever have envisioned. Most of them wished they had never even tried heroin or "turned a single trick." They also talked a great deal about how hurt they were by the fact that the male clients at the clinic considered them "untouchable," or "damaged goods." At first I thought the women were exaggerating. But I discovered how right they were when I overheard a group of male clients declaring loudly that most of the women at the clinic were disgusting because so many of them had worked—or were still working—as prostitutes.

As I mentioned earlier, every time prostitutes and their customers have sex, they place one another and all of their other sexual partners at risk for sexually transmitted diseases. This is especially true when condoms are not used, but it is even true when they are used, since there is always a chance that the condoms could slip off or break. I once heard a radio news program that featured an HIV-positive, drug-addicted woman speaking to a reporter about why she was still working as a prostitute. She rationalized her behavior as follows: "I'm sorry. I know it's wrong. But no one else gives a damn if I live or I die. I have to look out for 'number one.' It's better than robbing people. My friends say I might be charged with attempted murder if I get caught, but that's just a chance I have to take. I can't worry about other people. I have to make enough money to get my drugs. If you'd ever been 'dope-sick' you'd know what I mean. How's a straight guy like you ever going to understand where I'm coming from? If I don't get my drugs, I'll die. And if I do get my drugs, I'll die. I don't care about the dying. I only care about getting rid of the pain that I'm in every minute of the day."

Thankfully, some of our female clients who had once worked as prostitutes abandoned prostitution as soon as they became fully engaged in treatment. Once they stopped using drugs, they no longer felt the pressure to raise large quantities of cash in short periods of time. They also stopped dressing scantily, toned down their make-up and hairstyles, and started to treat themselves and others with more respect. Once they stopped viewing themselves as commodities, they became less cynical and more hopeful. They also felt an empowering sense of control over their own destinies, a feeling they had not experienced in a long, long time.

12

Pimps and Dealers

I must confess that I felt somewhat less compassion for the pimps and dealers at the clinic than I did for the prostitutes. Hostility radiated from the men who worked as pimps like heat from molten lava. Their facial expressions told me all I needed to know—that as a young woman, I had less than nothing to offer them in the way of counseling.

That said, however, I have to concede that these men had not been born monstrous; they had been made monstrous by their life circumstances. Much like the women they were exploiting, most of them had been horribly abused and neglected as children. They had also been starved of positive male role models. The constellation of all these negative forces had caused them to grow up with a skewed notion of what it means to be a "real man." And the pimps at the clinic were men of relative power, at least in the culture of the streets, the only culture that mattered in their eyes.

There are not many non-criminal ways for an ambitious man in the underclass to rise to a position of power. The earning potential of a successful pimp can match that of a doctor or a lawyer in the straight world. In addition, in the underclass, money equals power, regardless of how that money has been acquired. In the drug culture, a pimp is a man to be reckoned with, a man to be both respected and feared.

As young boys, they had learned the cruel, Machiavellian "kill-or-be-killed" reality of life on the streets. In essence, a boy coming of age in that environment can become one of two things: an exploiter or a victim—predator or prey. They see few options in between these two extremes. Accordingly, many of them choose the surest path to survival, the predatory life of pimping, or dealing, or both.

In the final analysis, life in the mainstream may not really be so different. There are certainly plenty of predators and victims in society's middle and upper classes. It is just that people who are not in the underclass have many more options in life. It is a middle-class luxury, for instance, to become a social worker, as I did, since clinical social work is a career path that requires money, time, and a graduate education. There are few legitimate opportunities, however, for an ambitious man born into abject poverty to "make something of himself."

Many of the clients shared my disdain for dealers, particularly those who sell drugs to children, and those who do not use drugs themselves but merely make money by exploiting the chemical dependence of heroin addicts. When the news story first broke about a group of Texas teenagers who overdosed on black tar heroin and died, my clients became extremely upset. They mourned for those teenagers as if they were once again mourning the death of their own innocence. My clients had not realized it at the outset, but looking back, a number of them could see that they had started out exactly like those Texan teens. They, too, had first been corrupted at a young age by unscrupulous dealers.

Drug dealers know that it can be very profitable to cultivate—or rather, enslave—young customers. Initially, they feed their newest customers a steady supply of free drugs. It is only when these new users have become helplessly hooked that the dealers exact their first pound of flesh. Some young addicts are forced to pay for their drugs with sexual services, but most dealers prefer their payments to come in the form of cold, hard cash. The most grotesque aspect of this sort of "young blood" dealing is the fact that many dealers seem to take a sadistic pleasure in profiting from the misery of their inexperienced teenage customers.

It was understandably hard for our clients to think about those early days. But they believed it was important to remember, because those painful memories made them realize that the dealers who had helped get them hooked on drugs when they were very young were at least partly responsible for some of the terrible experiences they were now enduring as adults.

13

Methadone and Pregnancy

It goes without saying that the subject of pregnant substance abusers is a touchy one. And I always found it unsettling when female clients at the clinic who were still actively prostituting and using drugs intentionally became pregnant. I had trouble understanding why they would want to bring yet another child into a life of poverty and hardship. I should add, however, that I also knew it was not my job to express my opinion or to judge. I was there only to listen, and to offer my support and understanding.

As we know, women get pregnant for any number of reasons. Some do so in the hope of finding in their children the unconditional love they were never able to find in their relationships with men. This appeared to be the case with many of the pregnant clients at the clinic.

The clinic doctors always maintained that from a medical vantage point, methadone treatment is a perfectly safe option for mother and child. But I got a different impression from the nurses and child welfare workers who monitored and cared for these newborns in hospital wards. First of all, many babies born to methadone-addicted women are themselves addicted to methadone. This means that such children start life requiring immediate methadone detoxification, a brutal process for an adult, and a potentially life-threatening one for a tiny infant.

I quickly learned that not all methadone clients stop taking drugs just because they discover that they are pregnant. A baby born to a mother who is not only taking methadone, but who is also abusing heroin, cocaine, alcohol and/or other drugs, will likely be born addicted to all of these drugs as well. Therefore, at the moment of birth, the newborn will be in a painful state of withdrawal from multiple drugs. And infants withdrawing from several drugs at the same time are in grave danger of sustaining injury from the heavy stress this places on their small, developing systems. Additionally, a number of the pregnant clients at the clinic did not receive adequate pre-natal care (even though the counselors strongly encouraged them to do so). As a result, some of their children were born prematurely, a condition that can create a whole separate set of medical problems.

Many of the pregnant women we saw at the clinic were also coping with multiple psychosocial and medical issues, such as spousal abuse, prostitution, homelessness, and AIDS. The doctors at the clinic informed the counselors that when an HIV-positive woman undergoes a Caesarean delivery, the chances of her baby being born HIV-positive are dramatically reduced (though not totally eliminated). However, even if the baby of an HIV-positive addict is born without the virus, if that newborn's mother develops full-blown AIDS soon after giving birth, or if she continues to abuse drugs or work as a prostitute, she may not live long enough to care for her baby in the years to come.

Whenever I learned that an HIV-positive, homeless, actively prostituting and drug-abusing client at the clinic had deliberately become pregnant, it was hard for me to fathom why. I always tried to put myself in her shoes, but it was difficult not to feel some anger and shock, because in all likelihood these children would be born prematurely, addicted to numerous drugs, and in generally poor health.

I admit that I was looking at my clients' behavior through the filter of my own middle-class value system. I could not help but wonder what chance at happiness or good health these little babies had. What were the odds of these mothers living to see their children's fifth birthday?

As I saw my role, one of my primary duties as a therapist was to provide my clients with a near-constant barrage of "reality checks." I never told my clients how to live; my job was not to make their decisions for them. But I always encouraged them to think before they acted. And if a client appeared to be on the brink of making a decision that was going to make her life even more difficult than it already was, I strongly urged her to weigh all of her options very carefully before making her final decision.

Perhaps it would be advisable for more pregnant methadone clients to check themselves into the detoxification ward of a hospital, rather than continue to seek treatment at a methadone clinic. In the hospital, these women could be very gradually weaned off the methadone, as well as any other drugs they might have in their systems. Within the confines of a hospital setting, such clients would presumably not have access to illicit substances (unless their visitors secretly brought them illegal drugs).

Of course, it would be ideal if clients could complete this extremely tapered detoxification process within the framework of the nine-month gestation period. That way, their babies would not be born addicted to methadone (or to any other drugs, for that matter). However, even if a client's methadone detoxification process could not be completed during her pregnancy, a partial detoxification would be better than none at all, because it would make her infant's methadone detoxification process considerably less brutal. Of course, I realize that there are numerous logistical and financial obstacles that would make it difficult for all pregnant drug abusers to be hospitalized for the entire duration of their pregnancies. I still believe, however, that hospitalization, or some other form of inpatient treatment, is a preferable treatment modality for many pregnant addicts.

14

The Children of
Methadone Clients

One day I had an enlightening telephone conversation with Ellen, a child welfare worker from the Department of Social Services. It turned out, though I did not realize it at the time, that this call presaged a major change in my life as a social worker. It was one of those unexpected (yet pivotal) moments that happen only a few times in a lifetime.

I never met Ellen face-to-face, but I would have liked to, because I was very impressed by the depth of her convictions. Among other things, she believed very strongly that there is never a valid reason to bring a young child to a methadone clinic. She maintained that if parents must go for methadone treatment, then they should find someone to take care of their children while they are away from home.

Furthermore, Ellen felt that methadone clients with children, who are either unable or unwilling to arrange for childcare, should simply admit that they are unfit parents, and voluntarily turn their children over to the state. This, of course, is not the "Black Letter of the Law," only the humble opinion of one very angry child welfare worker who had seen too many neglected and abused children suffering at the hands of drug-addicted parents.

After Ellen shared some of her views with me, I heard myself saying: "Oh, a methadone clinic is not the absolute worst place in the world to bring a child." But inside I heard myself saying: "Yes! You said it!"

She was right. A methadone clinic is a horrible place for a child. These children were exposed to cursing and vulgarity and about a hundred other nasty sights and sounds (including the occasional drug transaction). Beyond that, they have to see heavily intoxicated adult strangers on a daily basis. What a negative experience for a young child! Sad to say, some of the children had grown up with methadone clinics in their lives, because their mothers had been in treatment since before their birth. Some of them were as familiar with clinic life as they were with their schools and neighborhoods. It was very disturbing for me to learn that a methadone clinic could be such a big part of a child's everyday reality.

Amazingly enough, most of these children seemed remarkably resilient, or at least they seemed willing to make the best of a difficult situation. (Of course, they had little to compare it with, so they could not really know how difficult their situation was.) For the most part, they played together quite peaceably in the clinic's makeshift toy room, just as if they had come there to attend an after-school program.

I must also point out that the clients were not happy about bringing their children to the clinic. They certainly did not want them exposed to the terrible events and circumstances that they had witnessed as children. Unfortunately, many clients felt cornered. Not only was it a real challenge for them to pay for childcare, but also many of them had been abused when they were children, hence had difficulty trusting other adults around their own children. While I could understand that there were genuine obstacles preventing them from seeking childcare, I thought that some of them could have tried harder to do so.

It should come as no surprise that Ellen also had a very strong opinion about methadone clients who become pregnant. She said: "Do whatever you want with your own body. You're a grown woman, and I'm a libertarian. Feel free to poison your own bloodstream. I honestly don't care. But the minute a baby comes into the picture, I change my tune. That baby never asked to be born, so don't you dare go ruining its life just because you have problems. No drugs. Not even methadone! It's just too risky." She then echoed what several maternity ward nurses had already told me when she added: "I don't like to see those babies born hooked on methadone. They're always premature, and they're usually sick for a long time. It's simply unforgivable." She had visited far too many of these tiny, ailing infants in hospital wards all over the city, so she knew firsthand the havoc that even a legal drug like methadone can wreak on a small, developing body.

I was just beginning to appreciate how deeply conflicted I felt about working as a methadone counselor. Ellen's criticisms so closely mirrored my own that I suddenly felt as if I had met a kindred spirit on the telephone. I wanted to feel as good about my work as I could tell she felt about hers, but the more time I spent at the clinic, the worse I felt. A complete stranger had confirmed something I had already known in my heart, but had not fully admitted to myself until then: I still wanted to work as a counselor, but not as a methadone counselor.

I had been at the clinic a mere eight months when I took that fateful phone call from Ellen, but already I had grown bone-weary of struggling with all the moral ambiguities inherent in methadone counseling. In fact, she made me wish all the more that I had begun my social work career by counseling the victims of child abuse or domestic violence. As stressful as Ellen's job surely was, at least she could say in all honesty that she was working on the side of justice. She was a "protector of the innocent."

The oddest part about that phone call was that Ellen would never know how deep an impression she made on me. In fact, the full impact of her words did not become clear to me until a few days later, when I was describing the call to my husband and friends. I told them exactly how this phone conversation had forced me to stand back, take stock of my values, and honestly assess whether or not I was being true to my deepest beliefs in my work. It was not particularly pleasant for me to realize that I was not. Even so, I am deeply thankful for the phone call and its aftermath, because they enabled me to understand the cognitive and emotional dissonance I had been experiencing for some time.

The more I reflected on what Ellen had said, the angrier I felt at all the "non-compliant clients" at the clinic (especially the ones with children). They paid lip service to how much they wanted to straighten themselves out, but obviously they did not want to change badly enough to stop using drugs once and for all. I am not referring to our clients who were honestly trying to quit. I am thinking, rather, about a particular segment of the client population, the ones who still got their thrills from the "junkie" lifestyle, from the hustling and wheeling and dealing.

Back in their pre-methadone days, when their physical dependence on heroin had forced them to buy drugs, these non-compliant clients had come to despise the drug chase with a passion. Now that their bodies no longer craved heroin, however, the chase for heroin and other drugs had become kind of fun again—almost like a game, or a weekend hobby. In other words, for the uncommitted, non-compliant clients, methadone treatment had merely made the procurement of heroin a sport, a luxury rather than a necessity.

The more I observed the children at play in the toy room or in the reception area, the more I saw how watchful and vigilant they needed to be just to get by. They seemed almost telepathically attuned, for instance, to the slightest shift in their parents' moods. And they also knew exactly when their parents were using drugs, and when they were managing to stay clean. The tension from all this hyper-vigilance showed in their drawn little faces. Most of the clients claimed they did not use drugs in front of their children, but no doubt they slipped up once in a while. Considering how frightening it is for children to see a stranger nodding out, imagine how much scarier it is for them to see Mommy or Daddy stumbling around the house like zombies.

Many of the children bore the manifest signs of neglect, most notably, the sallow complexions and skinny limbs one associates with malnutrition. One of the saddest sights at a methadone clinic is a "parentified" child. An example of such a child would be a little boy who pushes his baby sister's stroller, changes her diapers, and feeds her. He is forced to perform these tasks, because his mother is too high to perform them herself. This same little boy might have to grab a burning cigarette from his dozing mother's hand before she unwittingly burns a hole in her own flesh or starts a fire. Incidents like that are all in a day's work for the child of an opiate addict.

Whenever I saw a "parentified" child at the clinic, my heart broke, but I also became incensed. Addicts often wonder why people disdain them, and I think much of the public's ill will springs from the perception that at least some drug addicts mistreat their children (whether they mean to do so or not). "John Q. Public" does not care why adult addicts behave as they do. He only cares about the children who may be suffering as a result of those addicts' negligence.

Whenever something seemed seriously amiss with a child, I was legally obligated to report this fact to the Department of Social Services. (Actually, my filing of one such report is what led to my fateful phone conversation with Ellen.) Any time we red-flagged a case for the Department of Social Services, one of their caseworkers would visit the client's home. There they would assess the overall situation, including whether or not the children appeared to be in any imminent danger. Sometimes children were removed from their homes, and other times they were not, depending on the caseworker's findings. The decisions made by the Department of Social Services often seemed quite arbitrary to outside observers like my colleagues and myself. Consequently, we always found it hard to predict which children would be placed in foster care, and which would not.

Seeing children with parents who were still getting high was hard enough, but suspecting that some of the parents were still actively prostituting, stealing, or dealing was even worse. I hated to think about the kinds of people who might be coming into their homes. I also worried about the bad habits the children could be picking up from observing their parents in action. How can a child who grows up seeing his parents break all the rules of civilized society learn how to distinguish between right and wrong?

Whenever I saw children walk into the clinic, I wondered how they could look so sweet and undamaged despite all that they had endured. There were even times when I had to look away from their innocent faces because I was afraid to glimpse already etched there what the future might hold in store for them. Would it be possible for them to overcome the odds and escape the fate of their parents? Was there even the slightest chance that they might manage to break the cycle, exit the underclass, and make the move into mainstream society? And even if they did manage to steer clear of drugs themselves, would they end up marrying substance abusers like their parents in a classic "repetition compulsion"?

I worked with a wonderful colleague, Ben, whose wife had recently given birth to a baby girl. He often spoke about how he could never imagine bringing his daughter to work with him. As a new father, it pained him to think about all those babies and toddlers being brought into the clinic every single day, even in foul weather.

The children's smiles shone like miniature beacons of hope, a small hint of something good and sacred amid so much that was corrupt and profane. It was hard to comprehend how something so innocent and pure could even exist in a place of such darkness and despair, but children in methadone clinics are like children everywhere. They are the living embodiment of their parents' best efforts, which is all the more reason for them to be spared the terrible sights and sounds of a methadone clinic.

I remember catching the end of a television news program that featured a tragic family scene that haunts me to this day. The father, blind drunk, had trashed his family's living room, then run out of the house. In his wake, he left shattered dishes, broken table legs, and a slashed couch. It was Christmas-time, and he had knocked the tree over on its side and dragged it across the floor, smashing most of the ornaments.

The police had been summoned and the mother, looking totally dazed, was telling them what had happened. She and the police officers were in the background of the scene and her ten-year-old son was in the foreground. He was frantically sweeping all the debris into a dustpan, and what became instantly and painfully clear from his frenzied activity was his determination to restore order to his home as quickly as possible. The policemen kept glancing over in his direction. One of them finally urged the child to take a break. This officer looked at the boy with deep affection and sorrow, but the boy was oblivious to everything around him, even the officer's sympathetic gaze.

No matter how much the boy was encouraged to stop, he would not be distracted from his task.

Whenever I recall the televised image of that frantic child, I also remember the tiny faces of the children I met at the clinic. After all, his story was their story. The children of alcoholics and drug addicts spend their whole lives cleaning up after their parents, growing old before they have the chance to grow up. I actually observed the aging process in their small, hooded eyes: that tragic mixture of courage, determination, and deep-down soul-exhaustion.

Fortunately, not all methadone clinics allow clients to bring their children with them to treatment. As a matter of fact, some program administrators insist that clients make all of the appropriate childcare arrangements if they want to participate in treatment. For the sake of all the children of methadone clients, I hope that one day all methadone clinics will adopt such a policy. It is vitally important that young children not be exposed to the kinds of conversations and behaviors that are commonplace at methadone clinics.

15

The Harm Reduction Treatment Model

I worked with three types of methadone clients: those who were completely successful; those who made little or no progress toward recovery; and, the vast majority, those who fell somewhere in between. The most successful type of methadone client is one who gets off methadone completely, and never relapses on illicit drugs. Unfortunately, this is not very common. According to my more experienced colleagues, of all the clients who manage to wean themselves off methadone, only a small percentage manage to stay away from all illegal drugs forever after. Either they resume methadone treatment or they go through a series of "revolving door" stays in detoxification facilities.

In the state where I worked, Medicaid had cut back from covering detoxification programs for thirty days to covering them for five days. Five days may be long enough to detoxify physically from heroin, but it is certainly not long enough to combat an addict's psychological dependency. Sadly, I observed that many clients who participate in these five-day detoxification programs relapse on heroin and other drugs within a few hours of their release.

There were many more examples, however, of the second type of successful methadone client, of the client who stops using all illicit drugs by staying permanently on "methadone maintenance." It goes without saying that this is a qualitatively different sort of success than the first type. Clients on methadone maintenance say they feel chained by "liquid handcuffs" to a methadone clinic for the rest of their lives, but at least they get back their self-respect. Those clients who stay on methadone indefinitely and abstain from illicit drug use are regarded by the staff as successful because they have finally cast aside their criminal behavior. More specifically, these methadone clients are no longer dealing, hustling, or stealing in order to procure drugs.

I observed that the single character trait shared by all the successful clients—both those who "detoxed" off methadone completely and those who stayed in treatment indefinitely—was humility. Each one of these clients had realized at some point that the only way to beat addiction was to acknowledge its power, and to abstain from drug use completely and forever.

At the other end of the methadone treatment "success-failure" continuum were the clients who mistakenly told themselves they could still dabble in illegal drug use. Inevitably, these were the ones who ended up spiraling down into full-blown relapses. These clients never even managed to produce a single clean urine specimen and they showed up only sporadically for their mandatory counseling sessions. The clients who fell into this category tended to regard their drug treatment as a joke. Hardened cynics, they freely admitted that the only reason they had gotten into treatment in the first place was for the free methadone. They did not care very much about achieving sobriety, and they were brazen about thumbing their noses at the system. The clients with this attitude realized that they would eventually have to leave the treatment program. But until that day came, they were determined to enjoy the free methadone.

Coming somewhere in between these opposite ends of the spectrum were all of the other clients. At least 50-60% of all clients fell into this middle category, and their half-hearted approach to their drug treatment seemed indicative of their overall attitude toward life. Some weeks they were fully engaged in their treatment, but other weeks they just did not have the energy or the inclination to care. The results of their random, weekly urine screens reflected their ambivalence. These clients could abstain from illicit drugs for three weeks in a row before relapsing. This meant that they could string together enough consecutive clean urine screens to keep the administration at bay. But they could never abstain long enough to declare themselves truly clean and sober. The potent high they used to experience from drugs was long gone, but the ritual of cooking the heroin, finding that vein, and inserting that needle into their flesh still had a very strong allure for them. However, they were using considerably less heroin than before, which was certainly a step in the right direction.

Some clinicians in the methadone counseling field believe that this behavior is not exactly acceptable, but the best one can expect. They contend, in other words, that a significant reduction in heroin use is an adequate "treatment outcome." They also think that to expect more from clients who lead such chaotic lives is to set an unrealistically high standard of behavior. For example, if methadone clients cut back from using heroin three times a day to using it three times a month, then in the eyes of "harm reduction" proponents, these clients have succeeded, or at least have performed "well enough" in treatment.

I am not denying that it is a noteworthy achievement for heroin addicts to reduce radically the amount of drugs they are consuming. However, I do not agree with the harm reduction advocates who say that this is enough of a change. I would contend, rather, that cutting back on drug usage is a critical step along the path to total sobriety. On the other hand, it is not an acceptable end point for any client, much less for 50-60% of all methadone clients.

Some proponents of the harm reduction theory also posit that it is enough of a behavioral shift for clients to commit fewer crimes than they did before entering treatment. They maintain, in other words, that if a client is no longer breaking the law as frequently as he once did, he can be considered at least "partway rehabilitated." The problem I have with this argument is that such a client is still committing some crimes, and this is certainly not a "good enough" treatment outcome.

Harm reduction theorists also believe (and rightly so), that from a public health standpoint, these "halfway there" clients have significantly reduced—though admittedly not eliminated—their chances of contracting HIV or hepatitis. This brings me to another problem I have with the harm reduction school of thought: just as a person cannot be "halfway rehabilitated," either in terms of his level of addiction or his criminality, a person cannot contract "half" of a case of hepatitis or HIV. That's like being a "little bit" pregnant. My position on this subject may seem too black-and-white on the surface, but when we talk about clients achieving total sobriety, or contracting the HIV virus, or living a criminal lifestyle, there really is no gray area.

In my view, the "harm reduction" perspective fosters a culture of "lowered expectations" for clients. If counselors consciously or unconsciously send clients the message that it is permissible or "good enough" to stop at the halfway mark in treatment, what incentive would any but the most self-motivated clients have to achieve total sobriety?

I personally felt duty-bound to convey a sense of eternal optimism and high standards to all of my clients. I believed it was my professional obligation to let them know that they all had the potential to turn their lives around completely. In retrospect, I am afraid that my determination to maintain my optimism was one of the reasons I burned out as quickly as I did. However, I could not envision working with my clients in any other way. To tell the truth, I could not have lived with myself if I had sent them the message that "halfway there" was good enough.

Recall for a moment the tracking system in schools. For the most part, we played out our assigned roles without a murmur. If we were assigned to the "average" math group, then we obediently gave average performances in math class, just as expected. Children will generally rise to the expectations of their elders, no matter what those expectations may be. They also tend to internalize those expectations, quickly labeling themselves and one another as "dummies," or "brains," or "average."

Most people who end up in methadone treatment long ago internalized society's view of them as "loser junkies" who will never make anything of themselves. Needless to say, it is a daunting task for a counselor to attempt to undo all those years of unhealthy internalization. Many of our clients seemed either unable or unwilling to change the way they thought of themselves, and I could certainly see why: it must be nearly impossible to redefine oneself in a positive light after so many years of being criticized harshly by parents, teachers, police, and other authority figures. Many of my clients had never been nurtured or encouraged to develop their inner resources; this, of course, was one of the main reasons they had turned to drugs in the first place.

To a certain extent, the harm reduction advocates are simply realists. I have to concede that. I just did not want to consider the possibility that some of my clients might be beyond rehabilitation, because I was determined not to become part of the culture of diminished expectations. Had I expected less than total sobriety from any of my clients, I felt I would have been sending them the same pernicious message they had been receiving all along. And I certainly did not want to echo all the other authority figures who had told them: "You can't do it. You might as well give up. Just forget it. You know you don't have what it takes to improve your life."

Perhaps I clung to hope because I witnessed some miraculous transformations in my office. I worked with clients who were mentally ill, physically debilitated, homeless, and jobless, but who still somehow managed to achieve sobriety and obtain housing and employment. While I can understand why some clinicians subscribe to the harm reduction treatment model, I discovered during my year at the clinic that I could not.

I remember talking about the harm reduction school of thought with Joe, one of my former classmates from social work school, who was also working in a methadone clinic, though in another part of the state. He said, "You have to be realistic. Your expectations are too high, and you're going to burn out."

I answered, "If I keep my expectations low, I think the results will also be low. I agree with you that I'll probably burn out sooner rather than later, but this is just the way I feel. I know that in my own case, I've always responded to teachers and other mentors who believed in me and pushed me to the next level, rather than the ones who just let me rest on my laurels. So I guess I'm operating under the assumption—correctly or incorrectly—that my clients will respond to the same type of approach."

"Listen," Joe said, "I think it's great to believe in your clients' capabilities. But you have to bear in mind what they've been through. I'm sure your clients appreciate your support and concern, but do you really think that your nurturing them now—at this late date—is going to be enough to make every single one of them turn their lives around completely?"

"I honestly don't know, but that's all I have to give them," I said.

"Put yourself in their shoes," Joe told me. "Say you're a methadone client. You're forty years old, and life has never, ever been kind to you. How much faith do you have in your counselor, or yourself, or anyone else for that matter?"

"I see your point," I said. "But I still think it's important to send the message to all methadone clients that they're capable of becoming drug-free, and remaining drug-free, for the rest of their lives."

16

A Clear and Present Danger

In my clinic, as in all clinics, novice counselors participated each week in an hour-long supervisory session with a more experienced clinician. Supervision is always challenging. However, in a methadone clinic, it can be even more challenging than in other settings. As I have already noted, some of my clients had fairly violent pasts, which terrified me. Of all my colleagues, my supervisor Marie probably heard the most about my various fears and anxieties.

Whenever I felt vulnerable or threatened—as I did a couple of times—I know that I could have called out for another counselor to come to my aid, but instead I froze like a deer caught in the headlights. One of the features of our clinic's layout that I disliked was the fact that we had no red emergency buttons in our offices (something that I'd had at both of my field placement sites in graduate school). Also, we had only two security guards, and they were both usually busy in the dosing area on the first floor. Clients were not searched as they entered the building, which meant that if an armed client had become irate on the counseling floor, we would have been utterly defenseless.

I was continually voicing my worries during my supervision sessions with Marie, and she was continually trying to assure me that the staff's safety was priority number one for the administration. Everyone said that if I ever had a particularly frightening client in my office, I should feel free to conduct the session with the door ajar. I hesitated to do this, however, because it could have resulted in a serious breach of client confidentiality. Although my colleagues were always trying to comfort me by saying that no counselor at the clinic had ever been attacked physically, my feeling was, and still is, that there is always a first time.

I also expressed my worries in supervision about working with clients who were actively suicidal or homicidal. I was grateful that none of my clients ever threatened to harm themselves or others. One of my professors in social work school told us about a time, many years ago, when he had been forced to address a client's homicidal tendencies. This client, a cocaine addict, would spend entire therapy sessions with my professor saying he was going to mug the next "yuppie scum" who walked by. Naturally, this client wanted cash to buy drugs. But my professor suspected that he was far more interested in terrorizing people. In his therapy sessions, this client described his fantasies about attacking "yuppies" in very graphic terms. He also said that he could never be sure when he was going to carry out his threat, only that he was definitely going to do it some day. Licensed counselors have a "duty to warn" both the potential victim and the proper authorities when homicidal clients name a specific person they plan to kill. This client, however, claimed to be hunting any random "yuppie," and his counselor, my professor, could not possibly warn every young man or woman wearing an expensive business suit that an unbalanced drug addict in his care had homicidal tendencies.

When I heard about this client, I thought of a little park near our clinic that was always bustling with young professionals eating their lunch and people-watching. Suddenly, these confident, well-dressed young businessmen and women seemed like such easy targets for any desperate, unstable addict with nothing to lose.

I was told on several occasions that the only thing to fear at the clinic was that someone might come in and steal the methadone from the dosing nurse. After all, the street value of the clinic's supply of methadone for one day can exceed a million dollars. Learning that someone on the nursing staff might be robbed at gunpoint did nothing to assuage my fears, and over time all of this amorphous anxiety began to seep into my bones.

It is not that I expected our clients to behave like angels all the time. (I was naïve, but I was not delusional.) It is just that before I started working at the clinic, I did not realize how deeply entrenched some methadone clients were in the criminal underworld. When I told a friend how scared I was that an unstable client might assault me one day, she said: "You can't work under those conditions. It's like trying to conduct therapy while staring down the barrel of a gun." She was right. I began to feel less present, less "in the moment" with even my most engaged clients.

My other great fear—rational or not—concerned my possible exposure to blood-borne diseases. I was not especially afraid of HIV exposure (mainly because I have read that the virus does not survive for long periods of time outside of the body). I was also not terribly afraid of exposure to the hepatitis B virus, because I had been inoculated against that disease.

As I have mentioned, however, there is no vaccination for another dangerous blood-borne pathogen: hepatitis C. And from what I have read, scientists have speculated that the sturdy virus that causes hepatitis C may have a longer "shelf life" outside the body than the significantly more fragile virus that causes AIDS. If the hepatitis C virus can actually exist outside the body for a while, then exposure to the blood of an infected person could be quite hazardous indeed. For example, doctors often advise people with hepatitis C not to share toothbrushes or razor blades with loved ones, as it may be possible to spread the virus through the trace amounts of blood that can be found on such toiletries. As I have already pointed out, many of the clients at the clinic were infected with the virus. In the course of the year, my fear of exposure to hepatitis C only grew worse and worse.

The reaction I had when I interviewed an intake candidate who had hepatitis C will indicate just how fearful I had become about the illness. When the interview ended, he left his cup of water behind. A half hour or so later, I was doing paperwork when I absent-mindedly drank from his cup. I realized what I had done almost immediately, and I dropped the cup, spilling water all over my office floor. I then ran down to the bathroom and literally washed my mouth out with soap. Afterward, I splashed my face with cold water and wondered what was happening to me. (I realize that unless the infected person's mouth is bleeding, hepatitis C cannot be transmitted this way. But at that particular moment, I was beyond rational thought.) While it embarrasses me beyond belief to tell this story, I feel that I must, because my fears—both rational and irrational—played such a large role in my eventual decision to leave the clinic.

No client ever did shed blood in my office, but that did not stop me from fretting about the possibility. And I became even more anxious when I read an article about a medical student who had become so afraid of accidentally pricking himself with a contaminated needle that he had been forced to drop out of medical school.

If a client with hepatitis C had actually bled in my office, I should have been able to clean up the blood using all the appropriate precautions (rubber gloves, disinfectant, and so on). And even if I had panicked, or had been uncertain as to what to do, I could have enlisted the help of the nursing staff.

Yet I could not find any comfort in this simple logic, because phobias are inherently irrational (and a small-scale phobia is exactly what I believe I had developed at that point). Fortunately, I was able to "exorcise" my little blood phobia (and a few other related "demons") once I finally left the methadone clinic for good.

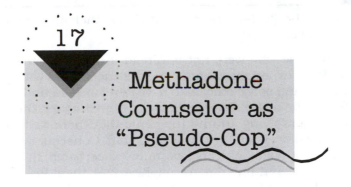

17

Methadone Counselor as "Pseudo-Cop"

I greatly disliked the fact that counseling was mandatory for my clients, because I wanted my clients to want to discuss their problems with me. If I had to twist their arms, what was the point? No one can be forced to bare his soul. If we are going to mandate that a client see a counselor, then we should not call it "therapy," because I do not believe that is what it is.

In addition to the mandatory aspect of counseling, we counselors were required to function as disciplinarians, or "pseudo-cops," with clients who broke any of the clinic's rules. This part of the job also upset me. If I had wanted a job in law enforcement, I would have gone to the police academy. I was trained as a therapist, a social worker. If I spent too much precious counseling time questioning my clients about missing therapy sessions or having too many dirty urine screens, how was I ever going to establish even a minimal level of rapport with them?

I am convinced that the ability to be a combination of disciplinarian and counselor is largely a question of temperament. If you are not "made that way"—and I am not—attempting to fuse the two contradictory roles just feels completely wrong. I never adapted to the role of "quasi-cop" as a way of regulating the behavior of my adult clients. Consequently, I had the reputation among the clients for being a "soft touch." Actually, because I was so afraid of confronting my clients who had violent histories, this was a reputation I had deliberately cultivated.

One of the most regrettable results of a counselor's playing the role of a police officer is that it feeds directly into the worst fears of some clients. Many of the mentally ill clients at the clinic were already suffering from severe paranoia, so when we took an authoritarian stance with them, their paranoia went into overdrive.

Even those who were not paranoid in the clinical sense of the word had experienced enough tense encounters with probation officers and police officers to have developed an understandable fear of the police. To complicate matters further, there were always rumors flying around the clinic that there were undercover police officers on the counseling staff. Consequently, when we acted like police officers, we only exacerbated the clients' collective fear that one day we might arrest them for real. For the record, none of us actually were police, but that hardly mattered, given the fact that the clinic's rumor mill worked overtime.

Ideally, I believe that therapists should serve as "consultants" to their clients, not as authority figures—and certainly not as gendarmes or "police impersonators." If I had had my way, I would have done nothing but help my clients identify their drug triggers and then brainstorm with them—in a truly collaborative process—about the best ways to eliminate those triggers.

In my own mind at least, my main purpose was not to act in an authoritative manner or to enforce rules. Coercing a person to change is never the solution, because forced change never lasts. And the thought that kept plaguing me the whole year I spent at the clinic was that I had been hired as a professional care provider and therapist, not as an enforcer of the law. In good conscience, I could not devote most of my time at work to regulating the behavior of my adult clients, and go home at night calling myself a "therapist."

I eventually came to the conclusion that it was not so much the clients I feared as the tense power dynamic fostered by the dual role we were compelled to play as counselor/disciplinarians. I did not want to behave punitively toward my clients, but I was required to act that way on several occasions. And whenever I had to act "cop-like" or authoritarian with non-compliant or potentially violent clients, I felt I was placing myself directly in the path of danger. This was not a pleasant feeling, to say the least.

Before I worked at the methadone clinic, I had interned at the outpatient mental health department of the Veterans Administration Hospital, where I had worked with a number of deeply troubled veterans. Some of these men had fought in Vietnam, and many of them were struggling with the ravaging effects of both substance abuse and post-traumatic stress disorder. These were unstable men with combat records and expert level training in the use of assault weapons. And yet I never felt afraid of them. I can see now that the reason I had no fear of the veterans was that I was never required to play the adversarial role of pseudo-police officer when I was working with them.

With the veterans, I had been able to function in that "consultant" role that I described previously. None of my veteran clients were mandated to participate in therapy. They could come to one session or twenty. It was entirely their choice. Whenever a veteran decided he'd had enough, he simply ended the counseling. No questions asked. It was just tacitly assumed that as grown men—several of whom had served as officers—they had the maturity to make those decisions on their own. There were never any power struggles to keep them in treatment against their will.

Moreover, in the sobriety groups that I co-facilitated at the V.A. Hospital, we employed the honor system rather than urinalysis. The veterans were very respectful, both of the system and of one another. No one ever came to a group therapy session while high. Maybe their military service had instilled in them a sense of honor, or maybe they just liked operating in a system that treated them like the adults they were. I should add here that while I did not work with methadone clients at the V.A., I did work with veterans who were battling substances other than heroin. This is an important distinction to make, because methadone treatment is quite different from other forms of substance abuse treatment.

When the variables of mandatory counseling and counselors being required to pose as policemen are subtracted from the treatment equation, all that is left is simple, straightforward counseling. Heroin addicts in need of counseling who have already been arrested a few times are not looking for one more adversarial relationship to add to their collection. They already have enough bona fide police and probation officers monitoring their conduct. What they need from their drug counselors is pure, unadulterated therapy.

18

Transference

I realize it is not quite this simple, but I sometimes like to think of transference as the unconscious tendency of clients to project images of their parents and other influential figures onto the faces of their counselors. The primary way that my colleagues and I maintained our "blank screen" status in the eyes of our methadone clients was by never disclosing any personal details about our private lives. This applied not only to what we said, but also to certain unspoken factors, such as how we dressed, or how we decorated our offices. Some of my married colleagues chose not to wear their wedding bands to work, because they did not want to reveal their marital status to their clients. Also, a number of them did not keep any photographs of their loved ones in their offices. I took the middle path in that I did wear my wedding ring, but I did not display any personal photographs. As an additional safety precaution, if we brought magazines or newspapers to the clinic from home, the administrators asked us to remove the mailing labels, so that our clients could not find out where we lived.

Many of the clients had been damaged in one way or another by their parents, so we were advised to take a sort of parental stance with them. The idea was to give them a "corrective" emotional experience, or to re-enact a facsimile of a healthy parent-child bond. According to this theory, when the clients had been younger, their parents had failed to establish appropriate limits around their behavior. Consequently, they had grown up longing for someone to care enough about them to set firm boundaries and help them stop living so recklessly. Theoretically, if I were to enforce all the rules of the clinic, my clients would come to view me as the benevolent (yet strict) "mother figure" they had never actually had.

This is a lovely idea at the abstract level, but in practice at a methadone clinic, it is another story. First of all, our clients despised the rules that we counselors had to enforce. They did not believe that the regulations were "for their own good." To the contrary, they thought the rules were for the staff's convenience. Who could blame them? As long as we were required to police their every move, we were never going to gain their unequivocal trust. Beyond that, not a single one of my clients came to view me as a "mother figure"—benevolent or otherwise—probably because I was at least ten or twenty years younger than most of them. A few of them stated outright that they viewed me as a "daughter figure," but that was about it.

Additionally, many of the clients were numb, too deeply involved in their drug addiction to feel much of anything for anybody, including their counselors. For transference to develop, clients need to have some feelings—positive, negative, or mixed—about their therapist. However, if prolonged drug abuse has virtually shut down their capacity to feel, then therapeutic transference can barely even begin to develop.

On the subject of "negative transference," whenever I sensed that one of my clients was angry at me, I felt like a miserable failure (which was probably yet another sign of my professional immaturity). A more experienced therapist would probably have known better than to take her methadone clients' transference quite so personally.

I remember some of my colleagues describing transference. They said: "It's not you they see in that chair. It's Mommy, or Daddy, or Grandma. But it's definitely not you. Remember, when they get angry in therapy, they are actually thinking of some other person, someone who is not even in the room with you. In fact, the person you are has absolutely nothing to do with anything that goes on between you and your clients."

Nonetheless, I was curious about what my clients thought about me as a person. Of course, they did not know me very well, because I never said a word about my own life in our sessions. But they had to feel something—anger, perhaps—toward this girl from the suburbs who obviously had no personal experience with their "mean streets." A fair number of the clients hinted that they thought of the staff members as sheltered do-gooders who worked as drug counselors as a means of assuaging their guilt for being born into lives of relative privilege.

Last, but certainly not least, is the question of sexual trans-ference. Did any of my clients become sexually attracted to me? And if so, how did it affect the therapeutic process? I must say, if any of them did develop crushes on me, they did not show it. They occasionally paid me compliments, but usually as a diver-sionary tactic to shift the focus of the session away from their own behavior.

In addition, years of hardcore drug abuse can significantly diminish a person's libido. With many of the clients, all of their sensory systems—including their sex drives—had shut down long ago. They could no longer be turned on by any stimulus as natural as sexual attraction. In many cases, the only thing that could still animate their deadened spirits was the artificial stimu-lus of drugs. Some of them were physically impotent, whereas others had simply lost interest in sex. Even the ones who were still sexually active never overtly expressed any attraction to me.

There is another factor to consider with sexual transference and methadone clients. Think back for a moment to a high school teacher you initially found handsome or pretty, but who was also extremely strict and demanding. After that teacher scolded you or criticized your work for the umpteenth time, his or her looks became something of a moot point. I think that is exactly what happens to many methadone clients. Their counselors pes-ter them so much about their treatment infractions that any spark of sexual longing they might feel in the beginning of treat-ment soon gives way to resentment.

19

Countertransference

According to the broadest definition of the term, counter-transference encapsulates the multitude of feelings that clients evoke in their therapists. And I must say that the countertransference that I experienced at the methadone clinic was complex and ever-changing. In some ways, I could relate to and empathize with my methadone clients' pain and hunger. In other ways, however, I had trouble grasping why they anesthetized themselves to the point where they could no longer feel anything at all—even good feelings.

Many of our clients lived in a state of perpetual exile from their own emotions, which rendered them passive and inert. They took their methadone, and they went to their counseling sessions, but they were not truly engaged in their own lives, much less in their drug treatment. These clients just seemed to be "going through the motions" of living. However, as tragic as their inertia was, it was also somewhat irritating, because it seemed so wasteful. Some days I would think about all the people in the world who were suffering from life-threatening illnesses like cancer. How much would a terminally ill patient give for just a few more days of "real life" with all of its attendant joys and sorrows? Most terminally ill patients would gladly rip out their mind-numbing morphine drips if they could be guaranteed just five more minutes of lucidity with their loved ones. But so many of our methadone clients seemed more than willing to throw away their real lives in exchange for these hazy, drug-tinged "shadow-lives."

One of my goals as a social worker has always been to give my clients "unconditional positive regard." It was true that many of my methadone clients had been mistreated by their parents. By acting kindly toward them, I was trying to compensate in some small way for their previous suffering. I also believed that by "accentuating the positive," that is, by focusing on their accomplishments as opposed to their setbacks, I could help them make some significant progress. In some cases, I believe that this was the correct approach to take; some clients did very well in my care.

Unfortunately, however, there were also clients on my caseload who were so resigned to their fates, and so paralyzed by anguish and chronic depression, as to be virtually immobilized. They seemed too far gone for my "cheerleader" counseling style, and they had no interest in identifying and then learning how to capitalize on their strengths. Also, they probably would have felt that I was mocking them if I had acted too upbeat in their presence. So I very deliberately "turned down the volume" of my treatment style in sessions with my most severely depressed clients.

In addition, a few of our clients seemed to have no respect for the value of human life. One time, I saw one of my colleagues walking out of a group therapy session she had been conducting. She looked ghost-white and close to tears. I asked if something had happened, and she said she felt nauseated. Her group members had been talking about killing people and how much fun it would be to buy guns to blow away all their enemies. She had repeatedly tried to steer the conversation in another direction, but the clients kept returning to the topic of guns. The discussion had become very graphic at times, and it had made her feel sick to her stomach. I never had a comparable experience. However, I did have moments when I wanted to tell some of my clients that human life is precious and not something to be squandered or taken for granted (though I held my tongue, of course).

As I have already indicated, I was frightened of those clients who had extensive criminal records. During our sessions, I tried to concentrate on the task at hand, but it was sometimes hard to maintain my objectivity and neutrality when I thought about the brutal crimes they had committed in order to procure drugs.

With the most violent clients, I sometimes fantasized about saying something along the lines of: "You're depressed? So sorry to hear it. You know who else is feeling a little blue? The guy you robbed at gunpoint so you could score your drugs. He's still having nightmares about you. And you know who else is feeling a little down these days? Your children, the ones you neglect so you can go buy still more drugs. So I hope you'll pardon me if I reserve the bulk of my compassion for all the people you're hurting as a result of your drug abuse." (Of course, I never said anything remotely like this to any of my clients, but the purpose of this chapter is to convey all facets of my countertransference.)

Beyond that, when some clients talked about how "boring" the straight world seemed, I was tempted to ask what was so fascinating about getting high every day (though again, I never did). To them, the idea of catching a movie or a ballgame without getting high first seemed incredibly dull. I realize that their attitude was merely symptomatic of their addiction, but nonetheless, it occasionally annoyed me.

The fact that methadone treatment has no set end-point also added to my sense of frustration. In this day and age—the era of managed care—long-term treatment for any condition is considered a rarity. For example, people are lucky if they can get eight to twelve mental health visits at their HMOs for the treatment of depression. Yet, as I noted previously, methadone maintenance can continue for the duration of a client's lifetime, an expensive proposition, to be sure. (Again, this is probably why so few private insurers are interested in covering it.) But at least with short-term treatment, such as the type now being offered by many HMOs, there is a built-in incentive for clients to try to "get well" as quickly as possible. One of my professors who specialized in short-term therapy often remarked that the reason she believed so strongly in brief treatment was that she did not want her clients to become too dependent on either her or the therapeutic process. Rather, she wanted to use the few sessions she had with her clients to equip them with a set of emotional tools and coping skills that would enable them to function independently in the world.

On the other hand, long-term treatment programs—such as methadone maintenance—can sometimes be detrimental to client care. Depending on the whims of the administration, a noncompliant methadone client may or may not be involuntarily detoxified from methadone treatment for breaking too many rules (often after being granted several months' worth of "second chances"). But otherwise, methadone clients have very little incentive to change their behavior in a timely fashion.

I was always being warned by my colleagues not to expend too much effort. They said: "Don't get 'over-invested' in your job. This is the clients' treatment. Not yours. They should be doing the bulk of the hard work." Of course, my colleagues were only trying to prevent me from burning out, but their warnings went unheeded, and I continued to expend too much effort and energy. In the process, my reservoir of compassion started to dry up.

In social work school, we spent a great deal of class time discussing the obstacles that stand in the way of clients' progress: poverty, substance abuse, domestic violence, child abuse, and so on. I am glad we studied those important subjects in-depth, but I also think we should have spent a little more time discussing impediments to successful counseling: the novice practitioner's feelings of emotional depletion and frustration, that dreaded combination commonly known as "compassion fatigue."

Now that I was out of social work school and in the real world of social work practice, I was hitting the wall of client apathy and the oxymoronic absurdity of "mandatory counseling." The clients always wanted to talk about the clinic's rules (despite the fact that they had much more pressing issues to discuss). Of course, if we counselors had not been required to act more like law enforcers than therapists, the clients would probably have been far less obsessed with the clinic's rules and regulations.

Like any eager new social work school graduate, I was dying to use some of the therapeutic techniques I had learned in school. I wanted, for instance, to encourage my clients to chart their negative thought patterns in order to identify and eliminate their triggers, and also to develop new ways of thinking and behaving. To my clients who were literate, I sometimes suggested keeping a journal, or writing a letter to someone who had hurt them in the past. They could either send the letter, or keep it, or throw it away, depending on what felt right.

I had other clients who were either illiterate or uninterested in writing assignments. They preferred to learn more concrete "anger management skills," such as counting backward from one hundred or punching a pillow. Still others were willing to try some deep breathing techniques and "guided imagery" exercises. It was always very gratifying when my clients actually tried and benefited from the "homework assignments" that I gave them.

Intellectually, I understood that our clients' tendency to idle along in neutral gear was only natural. Everyone coasts for a while before plunging headlong into radical life changes, so it was unfair of me to get so upset about what I perceived as their stagnation. I have often been guilty of the same "crimes"—stalling, hesitating, second-guessing. Making genuine, permanent change is a very slow (and often painful) process. And yet, as upset as I sometimes felt about client apathy and inertia, I was much angrier at myself for not being able to withstand the pressures of the job.

A friend once said: "You're a social worker, Rachel. Who did you expect to work with—happy, well-adjusted people?" Of course not. I just hadn't realized that my first job would be with one of the most challenging client populations there is. People had tried to warn me that this was a tough population to work with, but I hadn't wanted to listen.

When I consider all the ways I was not suited to this job, I could not tell you why or how I stayed for a full year. I suppose it had something to do with pride and my reluctance to admit the grave error I had made in taking the job in the first place. I was also disinclined to give up my shiny new professional identity as a "clinical social worker." It was a title I had worked hard to earn, and I didn't want to leave it behind, even for a while.

I also enjoyed telling people what I did for a living. I reveled in the sight of their shocked expressions. They said they couldn't imagine doing my job, and they went on and on about how "noble" I was to do it. I liked being perceived as brave (even though I didn't feel particularly brave). So for a while, I wore my job like a badge of honor. In other words, I did exactly what counselors often warn clients not to do: I began to derive my sense of self-worth from an external source—my career.

At one point, one of my colleagues and I decided to co-facilitate a stress management group. She was a very talented art therapist with wonderful ideas for teaching clients how to use painting, sculpting, drawing, and writing to complement their "talk" therapy. The group was successful, and the clients responded well to our exercises. Interestingly, on the few occasions when we tried to incorporate some very simple stretching exercises, most of our clients enjoyed moving around the room, but a few of them despised it. The body movements reminded them too much of the involuntary jerking motions that their limbs made when they were withdrawing from heroin.

After we held these groups, we always met to discuss the activities that had worked the best. Usually, however, these "debriefing" meetings turned into commiseration sessions about how to manage the stress our jobs were causing in our own lives. (We were pretty good at helping our clients manage their stress, but we had a lot more difficulty helping ourselves.) It was hard to go home in the evening and forget the horrible stories we heard from our clients all day long. Most nights, we were so emotionally wrung out that we had nothing left to give to our families and friends. In a last ditch attempt to remedy this problem, I tried to incorporate yoga into my daily post-work routine, but even that did not help. More often than not, I just went home and collapsed in a heap. Of course, this is a classic reason why so many social workers burn out. As a result of feeling emotionally depleted so much of the time, we sometimes find ourselves on the brink of despair.

Naturally, there were physical consequences to feeling so stressed out all the time. My stomach was always in knots. And at night, my chest muscles constricted and interfered with my breathing. My heart would beat wildly, as if one ventricle were at odds with the other. One night, the tightness beneath my sternum was so intense I became convinced I was having a heart attack. I remember glancing over at my slumbering husband and wondering how he could sleep so peacefully when my own body had declared war on itself in the middle of the night. Eventually, I could not take it anymore, so I woke him, and he calmed me down. It was not until that night of terror that I fully grasped the dire necessity of leaving my job.

Another feature of countertransference involves the client's gender. A lot of my colleagues preferred working with male clients. Many of the female clients had extensive trauma histories and personality disorders that made it challenging to treat them. However, I generally preferred working with female clients, because I felt I could relate to them more easily. Also, the female clients did not make me feel afraid.

For example, I had one female client, Fran, who had endured an unfathomable number of losses, and my heart went out to her. Despite all the pain she had endured in her life, she still saw the best in everyone she met. Some days when she left my office, I wanted to cry just thinking of her struggling out there in a world that didn't care whether she lived or died.

A few months after I first met Fran, she became very ill. It looked as if she might die, though she did eventually recover. Although I cannot disclose any clinical details about her case, I can share a brief, non-clinical anecdote about the day she cut a small tendril from a plant in the reception area. She just wanted to see if she could get this little vine to grow roots. Sure enough, she nurtured that rootless vine at home until it became a full-grown plant, giving me updates on its development all the while.

No one had ever bothered to take care of Fran in the way she took care of that plant. But amazingly, that is not what she chose to focus on in her life. Instead, she concentrated on making the most of what she had. Maybe that is why she impressed me so much. Not only had she survived a serious brush with death, but she had rebounded with such passion and energy that when she finally became well again, she seemed more alive than ever.

On the subject of positive countertransference, I find that I miss being one of the few people who was allowed to pay close, caring attention to my clients as individual human beings. When they went to the supermarket and paid for their groceries with food stamps, I was not the store manager checking their pockets for suspicious bulges, nor was I one of the other shoppers regarding them as walking stereotypes: "junkies," "welfare mothers," "thieves."

Rather, I was their social worker, their counselor, and as such I had the privilege of hearing their life stories on a weekly basis. At times, it was vicariously traumatizing to sit with so much pain. But when my clients opened up their hearts and revealed their emotional and physical scars, I was the one to take notice and care. And I remain deeply grateful for those validating moments of pure therapeutic connection that seemed to melt away all the barriers between us.

20

Working with Groups

Because of client attrition, my caseload was in a constant state of flux. The minute one client dropped out, I was assigned a new one. On average, I worked with twenty-five to thirty individuals and two groups per week. Of the two formats, I found group work considerably more effective and enjoyable than individual counseling, at least in a methadone setting.

When I look back on it now, I realize that group work is one of the things I miss about working in the methadone field. There was something very poignant about working with an assortment of ten or twelve people who had all been brought to their knees by the life-shattering power of opiate addiction. Their humility was awe-inspiring, and they forced one another to be brutally honest about what addiction had done, not only to themselves, but to their loved ones as well. I marveled at how much they trusted and confided in one another.

It has been said that laughter is the best form of therapy, and the people in my groups took that idea very much to heart. The last time I met with my evening group, we laughed so hard the tears rolled down our cheeks. A staff person even came to the door to "check on us." Raucous laughter—the sound of pure joy—is such a rare sound at a methadone clinic that no one knew quite what to make of it.

One reason the group format works so well for substance abusers is that they tend to trust their peers more than their counselors. When addicts are confronted about their drug abuse by their fellow addicts (rather than by their counselor), they are often more inclined to take action. When counselors confront

112 Welcome to Methadonia

their clients about drug use, on the other hand, they inevitably run the risk of sounding judgmental and harsh. Because of all the rules and regulations, there is an unavoidable "us-versus-them" tension in drug treatment, with the clients on one side and the counselors on the other. However, if trust and communication can be established, then this lopsided power dynamic can dissipate significantly over time, particularly in the group setting.

I had the good fortune of "inheriting" an established group from a counselor who had recently resigned. The members had been together as a group for many years, and they had seen numerous facilitators come and go. Perhaps because they had endured all these counselor losses as a unified group, they had bonded extremely well. They had adored their previous counselor—which worried me at first—but they quickly warmed to me as well. Soon I felt deeply honored to be a part of their "circle of healing," even if, as things turned out, only for one year. They allowed me into their lives, and I'll never forget that.

Several members were doing very well in terms of their sobriety, but what I most admired in them was that they were very modest about their hard-won abstinence. Even more importantly, they were very supportive of those group members who were still struggling to conquer their addictions. The successful clients always emphasized to their peers the vast importance of taking "baby steps" in their recovery process in order to avoid feeling overwhelmed—and also to prevent relapsing. Some of the successful group members used self-help groups, while others did not. However, none of the successful clients were preachy or self-righteous about saying that one path was better than any other. And their peers who had not yet achieved sobriety greatly appreciated the fact that none of them acted "saved" or "holier-than-thou."

Some weeks there was an almost palpable tension in the room, a negativity that seemed to seep in from the outside. During those sessions, the members acted uptight and withholding. But most of the time there were countless small but meaningful acts of tender kindness among members. On those nights when there was an abundance of heartfelt good will in the air, I sometimes left the room feeling as if I had been in the presence of something holy, something resembling divine grace.

Inside the safe haven of the group setting, the clients felt free to be their best, kindest, most generous selves. So many "good vibes" meant that none of them felt nervous about shedding their "tough-guy" and "tough-gal" personae, which highlights one of the terrible paradoxes of methadone clients: they may act tough, but underneath their hard veneers, many are quite vulnerable. Most had suffered terribly as a result of their tough-guy posturing, because they actually bruised quite easily. Indeed, if they had not been acutely sensitive people, they might never have felt the need to dull their emotions with hard drugs in the first place. When I think of an active opiate addict, I picture a baby bird with its mouth gaping constantly, because an active opiate addict craves heroin the same way a baby bird craves food: all the time. To experience a relentless, aching need of that intensity twenty-four hours a day, seven days a week, is to endure a life of hell on earth.

How can clinicians effectively treat clients who sometimes behave like hardened criminals, but who also have a soft, vulnerable side buried underneath all that bravado? I pondered this question all the time with my individual clients. But in my groups, the clients removed their tough-guy and tough-gal "masks" automatically, so I did not have to give the matter a second thought. For one hour during the week, they allowed their sweetest selves to rise to the surface. They supported and cared about each other enormously, and their caring was a palpable thing, as palpable as the anguish that permeated the rest of the clinic.

Outside the group setting, some of them were still breaking the law or disappointing their family members. But inside that safe sanctuary, where they felt profoundly understood, they could put all their scams and con games on hold. Inside the confines of this "womb" of their own making, they behaved like the people they might have become if drug addiction had not inflicted so much damage on their lives. They were not embarrassed about being witty, or well-read, or talented, or artistic. What was truly gratifying was that they could be themselves without worrying about being called soft or weak. In essence, they gave each other the time and space just to be.

The clients were not the only ones who felt liberated by the group format: I thrived as well. In my role as group facilitator, I let down my guard just as they let down theirs. Inside that co-

coon-like environment, I started—just barely—to sprout my wings as a professional counselor. The group therapy room was also my oasis, my shelter from the storm that raged through the rest of the clinic.

Best of all, it was the place where I could shed my hated "policewoman" costume, just as the clients could temporarily remove their tough-guy and tough-gal masks. I could cast aside the authoritarian role with my group clients, because I was not responsible for the "disciplinary" dimension of their treatment, which was the exclusive domain of their individual counselors.

The power, energy, and leadership in the room flowed from the clients rather than from me. Because I did not have to police their behavior, I could focus exclusively on facilitating their innate talents and fostering their personal growth. Rather than shaking my finger at them and pointing out all the rules they had broken, I could simply shine a light on certain self-destructive aspects of their behavior without the implicit threat of punishment.

In the same vein, because I was not required to "lead" in the conventional, authoritarian sense of the word, all the interventions I made in the group setting were gentle rather than adversarial or punitive. I loved playing the part of a true "facilitator." Temperamentally, it was the one role at the clinic for which I was perfectly suited. (Conciliation and encouragement come much more naturally to me than either confrontation or rule enforcement.)

If the group discussion strayed too far from the topic of sobriety, I sometimes urged them to stay on target. But I also sometimes encouraged them to engage in a few minutes of small talk, partly because they enjoyed each other's company and partly because I wanted to give them the chance to talk about subjects other than addiction. I felt it was important to acknowledge that there was more going on in their lives than just drug use. In this group, all the participants had spouses and children and jobs and hobbies, and I felt the more we talked about exactly what was at stake for them, the more inclined they would be to work on their sobriety.

My group clients taught me during these "small talk" portions of our sessions that it can be nearly impossible to get a job after serving time in prison. It is often just as difficult to establish a line of credit or qualify for a bank loan after finally becoming sober. Financial institutions, like prospective employers, are understandably wary of individuals with checkered pasts. And it is challenges such as establishing oneself as a viable credit risk and looking for work that can make it even more difficult for recovering addicts to maintain their sobriety over the long haul.

Most of the time, my group clients did not need me to "redirect" the conversation. If necessary, I believe they could have run their own groups, for the simple reason that they were focused on doing most of the difficult work themselves, which took the pressure off me. In this sense, working with groups was totally different from working with individual clients, some of whom did not assume enough responsibility for their own treatment. Inside the four walls of that group room, I felt no compulsion to "over-invest" in my clients' treatment, because the clients were already so deeply invested in their own treatment.

For instance, the clients in one of my two groups were so motivated and self-sufficient that they banded together to form a political movement of sorts. They did not want their names to appear on the test tubes containing their urine samples that were shipped from the clinic to a laboratory in another part of the state, because they did not want the lab technicians to know their personal information. The present policy, they argued, compromised their anonymity, yet methadone treatment is supposed to be completely confidential. As a group, they decided to send a letter to the clinic director. They gathered as many signatures as they could from other clients, requesting that identifying numbers (instead of their names) appear on the test tubes containing their urine specimens. From the beginning of the project to the end, they systematically and methodically planned and executed each task. They nominated one person to draft the letter, another to type it, and a third to collect signatures from the other clients. They then delivered the final draft of the letter, and later they received a written response from the director.

I resigned from the clinic shortly thereafter, so I do not know whether or not their action resulted in a change of policy, but I do know that the group members were pleased that the administration had responded to them in a serious, respectful manner. As their facilitator, I was deeply impressed that they had utilized the appropriate channels to pursue their goal. They proved that when they put their minds to it, substance abusers can organize themselves and fight for their rights as well as any other beleaguered group.

Only once did I fear that one of my groups might turn on me. When one of the newer members broke into a racist tirade, I told him that racist language was not acceptable. He did it again the following week. At that point, I consulted with my colleagues, fully documented the client's behavior, and then asked him in a private meeting to leave the group. I could not tell if he had been trying to antagonize or test me in some way, but that hardly mattered. After I expelled him from the group, the other members complained to me that the punishment should have been less stringent because there were no non-white members in the group, hence no one to take offense. Still, I stood my ground. Just when I thought I was on the verge of "losing" them for good, however, they rallied to my position, and the group became more cohesive than ever. In the end, the incident turned out to be a minor event in the long history of a tight-knit sobriety group that had been together long before I had arrived on the scene, and would stay together long after my departure.

When I left my counselor's post at the clinic, my group members expressed their gratitude and sincere good wishes for the future. Their kind words made me realize that I had not made a grave error by going to social work school after all. I will always be grateful to my group members. Not only did they show me what successful methadone treatment looks like, but they also confirmed my belief that a non-adversarial client/counselor relationship is fundamental to successful treatment. On the days when I was most inclined to lose my patience, my group clients rekindled my humanity, my faith, and my compassion. They also taught me that an addict's drug-abusing self is generally not his truest self, and that these two co-existing "selves" often have little—if anything—in common.

21
The Humiliation of Urinalysis

At methadone clinics, clients are allowed no modesty. There may be nothing more humiliating than urinating into a cup in front of a stranger—and on a weekly basis, no less. Many of our clients had nightmares about their urine tests. I once heard a news story about a sadistic male prison guard who tortured his female inmates by making them relieve themselves in front of him. He knew how violated and exposed this made them feel, and yet he persisted until his superior finally disciplined him. I also felt bad for the clinic's "urine technicians" who had to stay in these small, poorly ventilated bathrooms for hours on end.

A friend of mine who lived in Japan for a few years noticed that the toilets in public restrooms were constantly flushing. At first, she thought there had to be some kind of nationwide plumbing problem. Eventually, her curiosity got the better of her and she asked a fellow American what all the flushing was about. She was told that the Japanese are so mortified by the sound of "tinkling" that they flush repeatedly in public bathrooms (which gives a hint of how private the act of urination can be in other cultures).

In addition to the humiliation dimension of urine tests, lab error was also a possibility. Whenever methadone clients hand their specimens to a urine technician, there is always a slight chance that the specimen will be mislabeled, or lost, or even accidentally destroyed en route to the laboratory. There is also a chance that the laboratory staff might make a processing error, resulting in a "false positive" screen.

I noticed that no matter what happened, the lab always had "the last word." I sometimes questioned this rule, because I have known several people in my personal life who have gotten incorrect lab results at one point or another. After all, laboratories are not run by robots; they are run by fallible human beings. I realize, of course, that this "the lab is always right" policy served an important purpose at the clinic. Someone had to "take the fall" when clients disputed the staff's decisions, so why not let that someone be a something? It certainly was better to pin the blame on an amorphous, impersonal entity like a laboratory, rather than on an individual clinician, or a team of clinicians. Still, the policy bothered me because clean clients could lose their take-home dosing privileges as a direct result of lab errors. For example, clients with no history of cocaine use and a very long history of sobriety could have false cocaine-positive urine screens and lose all their take-home doses as a consequence. In such cases, common sense dictates that a lab error may have been made, but if the lab said it was true, then it "had to be true," and the clients were promptly penalized.

There is something terribly invasive and "Big-Brother-is-watching" about supervised urine screens. Some of the more anxiety-ridden clients became so agitated when they were asked to provide urine samples that they froze and could not urinate. I could hardly blame these clients, because many of them had documented anxiety disorders or prostate problems. And yet, because of clinic policy, we were obligated to penalize such clients for not being able to participate in the urinalysis phase of their treatment.

Moreover, a significant number of our clients had been sexually abused as children. For them, being watched as they urinated reminded them of the abuses they had suffered in childhood. Too often, the administration underestimated the power and toxicity of these traumatic memories, which meant that we clinicians were left to pick up the pieces in our counseling sessions.

Finally, because the urine screens were randomly requested, our clients often arrived at the clinic with uncomfortably full bladders. And in the cases of persons living with AIDS, or hepatitis, or prostate enlargement, this cannot be medically advisable. I worried that some of the unhealthy clients at the clinic were becoming even sicker because they often postponed voiding to be able to urinate on demand.

"Getting Over on The Man"

Not all of our clients had anxiety disorders or medical problems that made it difficult for them to urinate in front of others. Some of them simply did not want to do it. Consequently, the urinalysis system was badly abused by some of the more enterprising and imaginative clients. For example, if a female client was really desperate for a clean urine screen, she could purchase a urine sample from a clean methadone client and store it inside a container within her own body cavity. In so doing, she could be certain that the sample would be body temperature, rather than suspiciously cold to the touch. Also, to the observing urine technician, it would appear as if the urine were flowing from the female client's body rather than from a container that the client had inserted inside her body.

Our clients referred to the various ways that they beat the system as "getting over on The Man." And when I first heard about this particular technique of beating the urinalysis system, I could not believe it. But apparently anything can become a marketable commodity, given the right context. Wherever there is a demand for a "product" (even a waste product, such as urine), people are willing to provide a supply.

This was not the only way our clients "got over" on the urinalysis screening system. Some of them actually turned in fluids other than urine, like apple juice! Still other clients consumed over-the-counter herbal remedies to mask the presence of drugs in their systems. Many drank gallons of water in an attempt to purge the drugs from their systems. Some used drugs immediately after they gave their urine samples. (The specimens were requested at random, so these clients were gambling that they might not have to provide another urine sample for a full week, at which time the drugs they used the previous week might be undetectable).

Methadone clients have many other ways of "getting over on The Man." For example, a few of our clients were caught "cheeking" their methadone doses, meaning that they held their doses inside their mouths without swallowing. Then they carried the juice inside their cheeks just like chipmunks until they could spit it undigested into someone else's mouth in exchange for cash. Other clients at the clinic tried to obtain duplicate prescriptions for pills from different doctors. They then either sold their extra pills at more than a dollar apiece, or consumed the surplus themselves.

Bringing suit was another popular way of exploiting the system. A client might "trip" on a train platform and then sue the city, or the public transportation system, or both. The litigious clients felt they had been treated unfairly by life and that the world owed them some kind of recompense. Suing was one of the only methods they had at their disposal for wielding any kind of power in society. Unaccustomed to being in a position of power, when the opportunity to sue presented itself, some clients leaped at the chance. The notion of getting easy money out of some deep-pocketed entity appealed to them enormously. Some of my colleagues attributed our clients' litigious mentality to their exaggerated "sense of entitlement." I thought something else was also involved, a sort of David-versus-Goliath, "score-one-for-the-little-guy" sensibility. I do not know for sure how many of our more litigious clients ever received cash settlements for their efforts. But I do know that all those court dates certainly gave them a convenient way to avoid the hard work of getting clean.

At first, I was shocked to hear about the various tricks clients used to outwit the system. Some of their methods were rather ingenious. But what was even more dismaying was the discovery that—along with my colleagues—I, too, was "The Man." I hated being lumped together by our clients with police officers, judges, prison wardens, and other despised authority figures, but I was, and there was nothing I could do about it.

A tendency to deceive oneself and others is one of the features of addiction. In fact, many of our clients tended to lie not just about important matters, but also about trivial concerns.

On the other hand, when some of them finally got clean and sober, they also stopped telling lies.

I remember a colleague discussing Andy, a client she had treated who had earned his first take-home dose. He initially felt very happy, but a few days later he requested that she revoke the privilege, because he admitted to buying extra methadone on the street in order to get high. Andy's confession revealed that he was serious about becoming sober, because his methadone abuse was something his counselor never could have detected on her own. Our clients' urine samples were tested only for the presence of methadone, not for the quantity (and the clients were well aware of this critical flaw in our urinalysis system). So if Andy's dose was 45 milligrams per day, but he was ingesting an extra 100 milligrams every few days, there was no way his counselor could have known unless he confessed, or was arrested while purchasing the street methadone. He could have continued buying his illicit methadone and deceiving his counselor, but because of the progress he had made in treatment, he was able to break his pattern of lying.

Andy may not have even intended to confess that day, but apparently his desire to get sober had finally become strong enough to prevail over both his desire to use drugs and his desire to deceive. He was unhappy that his take-home dose had to be revoked as a result of his admission, but he also realized that he was not quite ready yet to handle the privilege wisely. By making the choice to re-earn the privilege honorably at a later date, he proved to his counselor that he had come a very long way in treatment. Andy's story highlights the intimate connection between addiction and lying, but it also reveals the equally powerful bond between sobriety and self-respect.

Epiphany

Ultimately, the time comes when all addicts have to decide whether they prefer the genuine peace of sobriety to the false peace of drug use. It's a choice no one but addicts themselves can make. An insightful colleague of mine once summed up drug treatment as follows: "A client has to want sobriety like he has never wanted anything else in his entire life, because it takes super-human strength to conquer a soul-crushing craving like drug addiction."

Once in a while, when all the stars in the cosmos line up just right, a counselor might be fortunate enough to be present at the exact moment when a client is having a genuine epiphany. In the substance abuse treatment field, an epiphany occurs when clients finally realize that they have "hit bottom" and need to clean up their act. Some of our clients referred to hitting bottom as "receiving the gift of desperation." It is tragic that a person has to hit bottom in order to achieve lasting sobriety, but that appears to be the nature of addiction. And for most addicts, having such an epiphany is literally a matter of life or death.

Once clients hit bottom, or receive the gift of desperation, or see the light, the best thing their counselors can do is become their number one cheerleaders. If, however, clients are not ready to say goodbye to their old lifestyle, no amount of counseling is going to change their minds. That's because one person can never force another to experience one of these epiphanies.

I may have felt that a client had hit bottom, but my opinion meant nothing. A counselor can talk about all the wonderful benefits of a sober lifestyle, but clients will not absorb the message until they are ready to do so. Thus, a drug counselor's primary role is to stay alert and be ready to bear witness to a miracle that may or may not take place.

It is a very mysterious and frustrating process for both parties, because moments of genuine clarity are impossible to predict. There is no scientific method to help counselors determine exactly who will "see the light," and who will not. Actually, that is not entirely true. My more seasoned colleagues explained that there is one factor that sometimes indicates whether a client has a chance of getting clean, and that factor is the client's age. Once clients turn forty or forty-five, they may undergo what might be termed an "age-related epiphany."

More specifically, as a function of the natural maturation process, some middle-aged addicts simply lose interest in using drugs. It is a blessing when it happens, but unfortunately, it is not an automatic occurrence. In other words, just because some addicts happen to be in their forties, they will not automatically "see the light."

I was always surprised by which clients managed to get clean and which ones did not. It was especially distressing to work with people who were doing well in other areas of their lives, but who simply could not or would not stop using drugs. A person can spend decades relapsing before suddenly having one of these epiphanies and getting clean overnight. With some clients at the clinic, sobriety was like an alarm clock going off inside their heads: one day they were using, and the next day they were not.

A fair number of clients who appeared to be drowning in their addictions made remarkable turnarounds as a result of epiphanies. As a matter of fact, some methadone clients manage to turn their lives around so completely that they eventually become substance abuse counselors themselves. I believe that it is the unpredictable nature of these epiphanies that makes substance abuse counseling such a difficult and uncertain undertaking.

I often heard other counselors talking about clients who had entered rehabilitation programs twenty, fifty, or even a hundred times before finally achieving sobriety. For example, Susan, the clinic director, once told me about an alcoholic woman she had treated years before who had finally become sober on her 134th admission to an alcohol rehabilitation center. Unfortunately, this particular client happened to die shortly after achieving her long sought-after sobriety, but at least she died sober. No doubt, it was stories like this one that gave Susan and the other veteran counselors at the clinic the strength and courage they needed to keep going year after year in such a brutal field. Indeed, if that client could get clean on her 134th admission, then anyone could.

I had the privilege of bearing witness to a handful of client epiphanies in my own office. It was startling for me to behold such radical metamorphoses in my clients. The term "epiphany," which has obvious religious overtones, accurately describes the individuals who experience these revelations, because they seem to take on a beatific glow. And in a very real sense, they have been saved. Saved from themselves. Saved from their own dangerous impulses and self-defeating compulsions.

This "amazing-grace" quality may also explain the use of terms like "higher power" in the literature of organizations like Narcotics Anonymous. When addicts are in the thrall of one of these epiphanies, they can in fact resemble a person in a state of quiet religious ecstasy. Indeed, those clients at the clinic who had this experience sometimes looked possessed by some force from the Great Beyond. Their eyes seemed back-lit by a mysterious inner luminescence, and their gestures became bolder, more exaggerated.

Edgar, one of my colleague's clients, experienced a stunning epiphany after enduring a series of unimaginable losses. Several of his loved ones died unexpectedly in the space of one year. Initially, Edgar feared that he would try to anesthetize himself from the pain with drugs, but he soon realized that he did not want to walk around in a fog during this exceptionally difficult time. As hard as it was, he made the courageous choice not to run away from his grieving process. He wanted to stay clear-headed as a way of honoring the memory of his relatives.

As time went on, Edgar grew even stronger in his recovery, always attributing his enormous success to the spirit of his late family members, whom he firmly believed were giving him the strength to stay drug-free. As part of his recovery, he made several radical lifestyle changes. For instance, he started exercising on a regular basis and eating much healthier foods. He also entered a smoking cessation program, and started going to sleep much earlier.

Rather than being defeated or paralyzed by a very trying situation, Edgar emerged from his grief much stronger. Before experiencing those devastating losses, he had not taken very good care of himself. But in the wake of his epiphany, he became more health-conscious and aware of the precious, fleeting nature of life. Seeing so many loved ones die unexpectedly had made him realize that he wanted to live for a long, long time.

I am convinced that one day, while I was walking down the street, I witnessed an addict teetering on the brink of such an epiphany. The man looked just like one of my clients. He was walking about ten yards ahead of me. I probably would not have noticed him if another man sitting on a stoop had not yelled out to him:

"Hey, Ron!"

At the sound of his friend's voice, Ron halted abruptly. He did not turn around, but just stood there facing forward. I think he was engaging in the inner battle that so many addicts suffer through on a daily basis: "To use or not to use, that is the question." Then the man on the stoop cupped his hand around his mouth and yelled his friend's name again:

"Yo, Ronnie. Get back here, man."

I could actually see Ron's knees buckling beneath him. The collapse of his will was a visible thing. After a beat or two, he turned around very slowly and walked back toward the other man. His raspy voice sounded quietly defeated when he said: "What's up, Mark?"

"Where ya been, Ronnie?"

"Around. Detox, actually. Just got out today."

"Aw, man. Well, do you need anything? I can hook you up."

At that moment, Mark (who was visibly intoxicated) seemed to embody the world of drug use. When he called out to his friend, he was like a stand-in for Ron's own addiction beckoning to him. The moment of decision seemed to last about five seconds.

Ron could have tried to recall the lessons he had just learned in the detoxification facility and walked on by, but unfortunately, he did not. It was a moment frozen in time, a sort of "aborted epiphany." Apparently, Ron had not "bottomed out" quite yet, so still another opportunity for turning his life around came and went, not taken. All addicts' lives are filled with just such moments, moments that are pregnant with the possibility of change.

When I learned about the power of epiphany in an addict's life, I lost any illusions I may still have been harboring regarding my special ability to "save" my clients from themselves. A firefighter who rescues a baby from a burning building is a savior, a hero in the classic sense of the word. But a drug counselor's purpose is not to save her clients. Rather, her role is to bear witness and offer support when her clients play the heroes in their own lives by saving themselves. Once I let go of the misguided notion that I was there to save my clients, I was able to do my job more effectively.

Mentoring

By now, we have all heard former chairman of the Joint Chiefs General Colin Powell and others extolling the many virtues of mentoring. For the advancement of his cause, General Powell appeared in a series of televised public service announcements. In these spots, he discusses how critical it is for each child to come under the caring tutelage of a nurturing adult. A mentor can offer a child guidance and wisdom while accompanying him to ballgames, museums, movies, and concerts, or so the theory goes. A mentor can also teach a child right from wrong, the value of a strong work ethic, and the importance of not drinking, smoking, or using drugs. Organizations like Big Brothers and Big Sisters have utilized the mentoring concept for years, often with very impressive results.

If a mentor enters a deprived child's life at a critical juncture and shepherds that child through some of the more difficult developmental milestones, that child stands a fairly good chance of succeeding in life. A mentor figure can be especially important when all the other adults in a child's life are uncaring, uninvolved, abusive, or neglectful. A positive role model can be a relative like an aunt or an uncle, a teacher, a guidance counselor, a volunteer, a neighbor, or a coach. Some children have several mentors, while others have none. Very few of the clients at the clinic had ever been nurtured as children, either by their parents or by parent surrogates. Emotionally speaking, they were orphans who had been forced to raise themselves.

And yet some of them had witnessed the healing power of mentoring inside their own childhood homes. I am referring here to those clients who had brothers or sisters who had been mentored. These lucky children—the siblings of some of my clients—were among the "poor but plucky" few that a coach or teacher had deemed worthy of help and guidance. Unlike their siblings (my clients), these boys and girls had managed to stand out in a way that eventually became their ticket out of the underclass. Maybe a younger brother had displayed talent as a painter and had been taken under the wing of his ninth grade art teacher. Or maybe an older sister had shown some ability as a dancer, and had been swept up in the attentive swirl of doting dance coaches bearing promises of scholarships and glory. These talented siblings were exceptional, the chosen elect, and as such, they were granted access to worlds that seemed forever closed to my clients.

The charmed lives of their "saved" brothers and sisters served as painful reminders to my clients of what they might have become had some caring adult dared to take a similar interest in them. I treated several such men and women: they had enormously successful sisters and brothers who had been handpicked from obscurity and poverty by supportive mentors who had lovingly helped to shape them into artists, writers, musicians, doctors, lawyers, and teachers. It is baffling to see two individuals from the same family ending up with such radically different destinies. My clients wanted to feel happy for their successful siblings, but they found that very hard to do. Who can blame them for feeling envious of their brothers and sisters whose successes made them even more aware of their own bad choices?

Some of the clients appeared to be seeking as adults the mentoring and guidance they had never been given as children. Fortunately, some of them found a facsimile of the mentoring they had always craved—and had long been denied—in their "sponsors" from Narcotics Anonymous. Within the context of Narcotics Anonymous, sponsors are recovering addicts with significant periods of sobriety under their belts who serve as role models and advisors for those members of Narcotics Anonymous who are still struggling to stay clean. Many dedicated sponsors make themselves available twenty-four hours a day, and this accessibility can be enormously appealing to people who have been deprived of any kind of special attention for as long as they can remember.

Alas, having a sponsor in adulthood is just not the equivalent of having a mentor during childhood. Some critical opportunities for growth have been missed and can never be recaptured. And even the most caring sponsor can do little to help an opiate addict who has not yet experienced his own private epiphany. Nevertheless, while sponsors may not be able to take the place of childhood mentors, they can certainly provide crucial encouragement to addicts who are serious about their recovery.

I know a counselor from a different clinic, Steven, who worked with a client named Janice who had not graduated from high school. Yet her sister, Patricia, had earned a bachelor's degree and a master's degree from two very prestigious universities. The disparity between the two sisters' fates seemed so extreme that it took Steven a long time to figure out why the two women had taken such divergent paths in life.

Finally, he pieced together what must have happened from hints that Janice dropped during their counseling sessions. Apparently, Patricia had enjoyed the tutelage of at least one mentor—a teacher, or a guidance counselor—who had recognized her writing talent early on, and had helped her to develop her formidable potential.

As an adult, Patricia had become a widely respected author. She wrote frequently about "the old neighborhood," a rough, impoverished place that she had escaped, but that Janice, her drug-addicted sister, was still languishing in all these years later. When Patricia gave a local reading to promote her latest book, Janice attended the event with an understandable mixture of pride, jealousy, and trepidation. It is disheartening to think that if Janice had been mentored as her sister Patricia had, she might also have had a chance to realize her dreams.

25

"Counselor Pleasers"

Unlike the unfortunate clients discussed in the previous chapter, some of the clients at our clinic *had* received mentoring as children. It was not particularly difficult to pick them out in a group of addicts, since their behavior was markedly different from that of the others. I came to think of these clients as the "counselor pleasers," and I could relate to them far better than I could to the non-compliant clients. These clients insisted that no one had forced them into drug use, and they did not want anyone's pity—I want to be very clear about that. The only thing they wanted was to please their counselors, and seeking approval is entirely different from seeking pity.

I knew what to expect from these clients, and I never felt I was in danger when I was with them. As I have already noted in Chapter 18, some of my clients viewed me as a surrogate daughter, a feeling that often gave them twinges of guilt and shame. Shame and feelings of guilt are not pleasant emotions, and a cottage industry of "shame-and-guilt-bashing" literature has sprung up as a sub-category in the ever-burgeoning self-help industry. Some of these books would have us believe that shame and guilt are entirely malevolent forces sent from the bowels of hell to render us helpless in the face of their evil power. I would argue to the contrary, that some degree of feeling guilty for one's misdeeds can help more than it can hurt, since it enables us to assume responsibility for our misdeeds. We have all done things we are ashamed of, but as bad as shame can make us feel, it can also motivate us to do better the next time around. In moderate doses, then—with special emphasis on the word moderate—I would maintain that guilt and shame can actually be beneficial in certain cases. It is only when these feelings take over one's life that they become destructive.

I had a friend in college, Lisa, who broke up with her boyfriend Brian over his unwillingness to learn how to control his outbursts of anger. He told her that he was powerless to combat his rage, because he had grown up watching his father fly into fits of rage. He also said he was not interested in exploring anger management techniques with her in couples counseling. Brian did not believe—or perhaps he did not want to believe—that he was capable of changing his behavior. Lisa had no regrets about ending the relationship because, in her words: "There comes a time when we all have to stop blaming Mom and Dad for every little personality flaw we have. Brian wasn't willing to 'own' his nasty behavior. He knew that if he didn't change, he would end up losing me. And that's exactly what happened."

Like Brian, who blamed his father for his own bad temper, several of the methadone clients—both those with abuse histories and those without—were caught up in a "victim mentality." Of course, the clients who had actually been abused as children were authentic victims. But even abuse survivors have to move beyond this feeling of "learned helplessness" if they want to make progress in treatment. The only way for a methadone client to achieve lasting sobriety is to say: "The buck stops here. I am the one who sticks that needle into my arm every day. Not my mother, or my father, or anyone else for that matter. I am the only one. And I am also the only one who can stop doing it."

The counselor pleasers may have been overly concerned about seeking our approval, but at least they had moved beyond "victimhood" and were motivated to change. What they needed to focus on was seeking their own approval rather than ours. The moment addicts claim full responsibility for their own drug abuse is the moment they take their first crucial step toward sobriety. Whenever my "counselor-pleasing" clients had dirty urine screens, or missed sessions with me, they became very upset with themselves. The first thing they thought was: "Oh, no, I'm going to disappoint Rachel." In truth, I knew that even the most conscientious of my clients ran the risk of relapsing; that's in the nature of addiction. Yet even when I explained this to my clients, they still worried that I was secretly fuming at them.

Nonetheless, working with the counselor pleasers was a welcome change of pace from working with the non-compliant clients. The criminal types were frightening, and the zombie-like addicts were a disturbing reflection of my own potential for inertia and passivity. Overcome by fatalistic resignation, the zombie-like clients seemed so disengaged from everything that they barely seemed alive. Unlike the enthusiastic counselor pleasers, they seemed to have no interest at all in the promise of a new life. They had lost too much over the years to believe in new possibilities, and they certainly had no need for the small gifts I had to offer: the cheerleading, the pep talks, the sympathetic ear. In fact, my efforts only struck them as futile and silly—too little, too late.

Not surprisingly, the counselor pleasers were among the few clients who had been given genuine affection as children. Consequently, they valued the loving relationships that they had managed to cultivate over the years. As some of the only clients at the clinic who still believed they had something to lose, the counselor pleasers strove much harder to succeed than the passive clients or criminal types ever did. I loved the fact that they were willing to work through their problems rather than run away from them.

26

Axis II Clients

I n the fourth edition *of The Diagnostic and Statistical Manual of Mental Disorders*, also known in the field as the *DSM-IV*, all psychological disorders are divided into five axes or categories. Broadly speaking, Axis I encompasses what used to be termed "neuroses and psychoses." Axis II includes the personality disorders and mental retardation. Axis III demarcates medical problems. Axis IV covers environmental "life stressors" like a recent divorce or a death in the family. And Axis V, the "big picture" axis, is the self-explanatory "global assessment of functioning."

Mental health professionals tend to view most of the Axis I disorders as potentially treatable. Addictive disorders fall into this category, as do the various depressive disorders. Even a severe mental illness like paranoid schizophrenia (another Axis I diagnosis) is considered significantly more treatable today than ever before as a result of advances in psychopharmaceutical treatment of the disease. Similarly, studies show that anti-depressants like Prozac® or Paxil® in combination with supportive "talk therapy," can work wonders for even the most severely depressed individuals.

Those clients who are deemed to have personality disorders (Axis II versus Axis I), however, are sometimes considered "hard-wired" in a way that is virtually unfixable in the eyes of numerous mental health professionals. Accordingly, some counselors attempt to "work around" Axis II disorders, rather than "heal" them. In fact, many articles and books have been written about the unique challenges and frustrations of working with Axis II clients.

Aside from Anti-Social Personality Disorder, which is considered exceptionally difficult to treat, perhaps the two most difficult Axis II disorders to treat are Borderline Personality Disorder and Narcissistic Personality Disorder. I worked with "borderlines" (those diagnosed with Borderline Personality Disorder) and "narcissists" (people with the diagnosis of Narcissistic Personality Disorder) over the course of three years, first as a graduate intern, and then as a counselor at the clinic. And I have to confess that I now understand my colleagues' frustration when it comes to Axis II clients, because they can be significantly more difficult to work with than those with Axis I diagnoses.

Borderlines, for instance, have a very fuzzy sense of self. They therefore tend to attach themselves to others in order to feel strong and complete. Most disturbingly, borderlines frequently engage in the frightening practice of self-mutilation, often referred to as "cutting." According to their impaired sense of logic, if they can make themselves bleed, they can erase the fuzzy, surreal feeling that they do not really exist. Notably, when borderlines cut their arms or legs or stomach, they are often not expressing suicidal tendencies. On the contrary, the underlying impulse driving a borderline's self-mutilating behavior is actually the desire to feel more alive, not less so. As with teenagers I have known, unless borderline clients are entangled in one melodrama after another, they do not feel fully alive.

Also, borderlines tend to have very intense, short-lived romances and friendships that shine brightly for a little while, and then burn out as quickly as they began. Further, borderlines are impulsive in a variety of self-destructive ways. For instance, many of them abuse drugs, or indulge in eating binges, or go on compulsive spending or gambling sprees. Still others engage in promiscuous unsafe sex with numerous—and sometimes anonymous—partners. They also tend to fly into sudden, uncontrollable rages at the slightest provocation. Borderlines engage in all these edgy, dangerous forms of behavior out of a desperate hunger to stop feeling fuzzy and to start feeling more solid and three-dimensional. If borderlines are not living life to the extreme, they tend to feel insubstantial, even non-existent. One can imagine the difficulties inherent in working with people with borderline personality disorder—especially when they are abusing alcohol and/or drugs. One minute, they think their counselors have all the answers, and the next minute they are convinced that their counselors are complete fools. This makes for a very rocky course of treatment, characterized by a few fruitful sessions amid a plethora of fruitless ones.

I always chose my words carefully with all of my clients, but with my Axis II clients, I exercised the utmost care and precision, because I knew how easily they could be hurt. If I said anything that could be misconstrued as even faintly condescending, I ran the risk of being banished from their psyches for weeks at a time. (And it is pretty hard to conduct therapy when the counselor is in "exile.") I also knew better than to tell my Axis II clients that they had been diagnosed as such. Knowing that they had been labeled as "borderlines" or "narcissists" would not have helped them; it only would have offended them to the core.

Narcissistic Personality Disorder (also common among drug abusers) is a little more self-explanatory. Most people have met a narcissist or two. These individuals typically have grandiose, inflated, megalomaniacal ideas about their own importance within the larger scheme of things. They also believe that they are unique and of a naturally higher status than the rest of us, and that they should be treated accordingly. Clients who suffer from this disorder seek a great deal of flattery and believe that they are entitled to special treatment by their counselors.

When I was an intern in graduate school, I worked with Jennifer, a narcissist who (quite typically) vacillated between idealizing and devaluing the clinical staff at my internship site. She also had some features of histrionic personality disorder. One time, Jennifer became so angry with some staff members over a minor difference of opinion that she declared she was going to "put a curse" on all of us. (A common characteristic of Narcissistic Personality Disorder is the belief that one has special powers, such as the ability to cast spells on people.)

During one of my supervision sessions, I asked Margaret, the woman who was then serving as my clinical supervisor, why Jennifer had become so disproportionately angry about such a small disagreement. She explained that many clients who suffer from Narcissistic Personality Disorder have "narcissistic wounds" in their psyches that are so deep and painful that they feel compelled to construct very elaborate defense systems in order to protect their fragile egos against future wounds. For this reason, many individuals who suffer from Narcissistic Personality Disorder tend to react in extreme, melodramatic ways to situations that other people would probably find only somewhat frustrating.

I noticed that both the narcissists and the borderlines at the clinic had a very powerful attraction to cocaine. This stimulant seemed to bolster their self-esteem and make them feel more complete, at least in a fleeting way. In particular, cocaine was the "drug of choice" for most of the female borderline clients that I worked with over the course of three years.

One reason they preferred using cocaine was that it caused them to lose weight, and when they were thinner, they felt more attractive. In essence, when these women were bingeing on coke, they stopped bingeing on food. Heroin makes everything go soft and fuzzy around the edges, but cocaine creates the illusion of bringing life into sharp focus.

From my admittedly limited experience, I would also contend that many Axis II methadone clients mistake the cocaine-induced illusion of sharpened focus for genuine clarity. I also noticed that many of the borderline clients at the clinic used both heroin and cocaine, but rarely did they only use heroin. They seemed to find the obliterating high of heroin by itself unbearable, because it only enhanced their innate sense of fuzziness. All in all, the Axis II clients at the clinic suffered terribly as a result of their substance abuse issues because drugs further skewed their already shaky perception of themselves and the world.

When a Client Dies

Working at a methadone clinic is not exactly like working in a hospice program, but death is a constant presence. Generally speaking, people are living longer with AIDS. However, this is less true of addicts living with the disease than of non-addicts. Because of their chaotic lifestyles, many HIV-positive opiate addicts tend not to take their HIV medications properly, if at all. In fact, the first thing many heroin addicts do when they are initially diagnosed as HIV-positive is get high. To complicate matters further, many addicts living with AIDS are also living with hepatitis. Indeed, this deadly combination of viruses can virtually cripple a once healthy immune system.

Many of our HIV-positive clients said they were not afraid of death. In fact, a good number of them seemed to court death by overdosing periodically and keeping extremely dangerous company. They liked the idea of "nodding out" or sleeping forever, and several of them seemed to envision heaven as one long, glorious high. What they feared more than dying itself was the pain associated with dying from AIDS. As we all do, they wanted to die quickly, rather than slowly and painfully. And many of them took even bigger risks after they had been diagnosed with the HIV virus than before.

In my year at the clinic, I met numerous clients who somehow recovered after teetering precariously on the brink of death. I also experienced one very unexpected client death. Prior to being hospitalized and dying very suddenly as a result of complications from an operation, Tom had not seemed ill at all. In fact, the news of his untimely death was such a shock that at first I had trouble believing the clients who were telling me he was gone. I could not really accept it until I saw the death notice in the newspaper. By addict standards, Tom had always struck me as quite robust and healthy. He was certainly not someone I would have considered a candidate for an early demise.

To communicate the news about Tom's death, a notice was posted in the dosing area. But that was all that was done in terms of a public remembrance, which seemed rather cold and inadequate to me. Especially upsetting was the fact that Tom had recently become sober and had begun working toward achieving some of his professional and personal goals. Clients who were newly sober, as he was, could be wonderful to work with, because they had rounded a significant corner in their treatment. As long as they kept their sobriety uppermost in their minds, they could begin to address some other equally important issues in their counseling sessions. So here was an ostensibly healthy client with a seemingly bright future ahead of him, and in a flash, he was gone. It seemed so unfair. (Tom's newfound sobriety later made me wonder if he had experienced some eerily prophetic feeling that he was about to die.)

I asked Ben, one of the more seasoned counselors, if it would be appropriate for me to attend Tom's funeral service, and he replied with a definitive "No." Earlier in his career, Ben had gone to a couple of wakes for clients, but he had never known what to say to the family members. It would have been a breach of confidentiality to say that he was the deceased's methadone counselor. This meant that he had to pose as a friend, but as a friend no one in the family had ever heard of or met. Eventually, he stopped going.

Funerals, in Ben's opinion, were for the friends and family members of our clients, not for us. In fact, many counselors consider it inappropriate for a therapist to attend a client's funeral. On the other hand, some counselors believe that in certain cases, it is acceptable to attend a client's funeral. In other words, it is up to each individual clinician to find a way to achieve closure when a client dies.

28

The Counseling Staff

I have already mentioned my former colleagues, but I would like to say more about them. Let me start by noting how much I respect my fellow methadone counselors. They are among the most caring, dedicated, and humane people I have ever known. The veteran staffers ably guided me through some very tough times, and my fellow novice counselors were and still are my friends, my comrades-in-arms.

Outside of the methadone field, a "veteran" worker is a person who has been at his or her job for fifteen, twenty, or twenty-five years. Methadone counselors, on the other hand, are considered "wizened old-timers" when they have been working in the field for a mere two years. Not many people can last for long in such an emotionally draining work environment.

The more seasoned counselors were just that—seasoned—which meant that they were unfazed by anything that took place at the clinic. A disturbed client could be running around issuing death threats and the seasoned counselors would simply take it in stride. They counted on their time-tested belief that methadone clients generally do not possess the organizational skills to carry out their threats.

Many clients claimed to be "connected" to the local branch of organized crime, and while some of them may have had criminal affiliations, the fact is that even in organized crime circles, addicts are usually considered unreliable. They constitute a large drain on their families' resources, and are very likely not on good terms with their relatives. Nonetheless, such clients would threaten to have us "taken care of" when we made decisions they did not like.

Once, a rumor circulated around the clinic that a disgruntled former client had hired someone to kill three of the counselors. Fortunately, nothing came of the rumor, just as the veteran staffers had assured us. For me, however, living under that threat for a few weeks was sheer torture. I lost a good deal of sleep and it took me a while to stop looking over my shoulder. The veteran counselors, who had heard every conceivable threat a hundred times over, were very patient and kind to those of us who were rookies, and they took our fears very seriously. I also observed that many of the seasoned counselors had exceptional crisis-counseling skills. Technically speaking, working in the methadone field is not considered "crisis work" because it is long-term, but in reality it often closely resembles crisis work, because there are always dramas brewing and fires in need of being extinguished.

Some of my colleagues, both novice and veteran, wanted to leave the methadone counseling field. In fact, the turnover rate for counselors at the clinic was extraordinarily high. We told ourselves that it is healthy to want out of an overly stressful job in the same way that it is healthy to want out of a bad relationship. "Why compromise ourselves?" we asked. "Why stay when there are other jobs out there that might not make us feel quite this stressed?"

At first, I worried about the fact that some of the counselors were in recovery from drug and/or alcohol abuse, while others were not. I questioned whether this distinction might serve as a vague source of tension among the staffers. Fortunately, this turned out not to be the case. Those staffers who were recovering alcoholics or recovering addicts were extremely open about their experiences, and they had many valuable insights and anecdotes to share. Because they understood the horrors of addiction at such a personal, visceral level, they could explain exactly why the clients behaved as they did. I remain deeply grateful for their honesty, their courage, and their willingness to share their stories as a means of educating others about the perils of addiction.

I thoroughly enjoyed the company of all of my colleagues. Some of them were particularly funny in a sort of dark, "gallows-humor" way. Also, they were all very knowledgeable and generous about sharing their accumulated wisdom. But when we ate lunch together, I felt that our conversations too often gravitated to the dark side. For some reason or other, some of my colleagues seemed to prefer discussing the more upsetting current events in the news.

I would have thought that people who worked in a methadone clinic would have preferred to discuss lighter fare at lunchtime, if only to have a respite from the darkness of their days. I certainly wanted to use my lunch breaks to "decompress" and temporarily forget about all the suffering in the world. In many workplaces, people deliberately talk about mundane topics at lunchtime in order to relax and forget their worries. This desire that some of my colleagues felt to talk mainly about the darker side of life made me wonder whether the pain and suffering at the clinic had gotten to them.

In addition, we were required to attend mandatory "peer support" group sessions on Friday afternoons, to give one another moral support and advice about clients. Sad to say, these meetings were often counterproductive. Rather than lifting each other's spirits, we often spent the entire hour talking about how difficult our jobs were. What bothered me the most was the idea of mandating people to "support" one another. (To me, it makes about as much sense as mandating clients to take part in therapy.) I think the idea of giving counselors a formalized opportunity to support and advise one another is truly laudable, but I also think it should be a voluntary program rather than a mandatory one. Inevitably, our compulsory meetings deteriorated into griping sessions, in which we complained about office politics and our salaries, rather than discussing more substantive issues, such as specific cases. We sometimes left those weekly sessions feeling even sadder and more overworked than we had felt going in, which of course totally defeated the purpose.

When I worked there, it seemed that several of the counselors were unhappy to one degree or another, in part because they felt they were being asked to do more and more work for the same low salary. And just as we counselors felt pressure to keep working harder and harder, our clients felt pressure from us to become totally drug-free as quickly as possible.

There were times, however, when I am afraid that we counselors became so caught up in complaining about all the pressure we were under that we lost sight of just how privileged and fortunate we truly were. It was too easy for us to forget that our clients would have traded places with any one of us. They would have given their right arm for just the smallest taste of our pedestrian problems, our ordinary, mainstream lives. While it was hard enough for us to sit with our clients' sadness and suffering for forty hours a week, at least we could go home at night and escape all that anguish. For our clients, there was no such escape.

That said, there were also many things I enjoyed about working as a member of a clinical team. For instance, while all of the more seasoned counselors made themselves readily available to the novice clinicians, there was one particular veteran counselor—Ben—who was especially kind to us. He really took us under his wing right from day one.

If an irate client yelled at one of us, or if we were feeling particularly frustrated about the high level of client non-compliance, we knew we could always turn to Ben, our mentor, to give us support, guidance, and a sense of perspective. He reminded us that we were not expected to work miracles, and that the clients were the ones who needed to do the bulk of the work in order to get clean and sober. He was patient, understanding, and soothing, an utterly non-confrontational person.

We all agreed that Ben had to be an exceptionally talented methadone counselor, because he always knew exactly what to say to make us feel better. Indeed, his clients did seem completely at ease in his presence. There are certain individuals who seem to be "born counselors," in the sense that they have a very comforting, easy-going way about them, and I would definitely place Ben in that category.

I once asked him, "After five years of working in the methadone field, how have you managed not to become totally depleted and burned out?"

He responded by talking about the different things drug counselors do to refuel, such as attending Alanon meetings, support groups for the family members and friends of alcoholics and addicts. (My supervisor, Marie, had also talked to me extensively about the many benefits of participating in the Alanon program.) "Alanon meetings," he continued, "can be very helpful for drug counselors because when you work with addicts, you sometimes feel like you are living—or at least spending eight long hours a day—within the confines of a dysfunctional, alcoholic family. No matter how hard you try to prevent it, your clients' pain starts to get under your skin. No pun intended. In a sense, it becomes your pain as well. Consequently, you have to find an outlet, some means of releasing all that pain."

"Do you go to Alanon meetings?"

"I have in the past," he replied. "And they were very helpful. What I do now is pace myself. I never expect miracles, so when they do happen—which they sometimes do—I'm always pleasantly surprised. Methadone treatment is probably the longest of all the different forms of long-term treatment. As you know, some clients stay in treatment for the rest of their lives. Also, not all of our clients make a lot of progress—and those who do make progress tend to do so very slowly. So I pace myself accordingly. That way I don't go off the deep end."

"But it can be so frustrating, don't you think?" I asked.

"It can be. But it's a lot less frustrating when you learn how to adjust your expectations to match the realities of the work."

29

A Flood
of Tears

On my very first day of counseling, a client began sobbing inconsolably in my office. I panicked. I did not even have any tissues to offer her. So there she was, tears streaming down her face, and there I was, sitting across from her in a state of shock. I had previously interned with veterans, who had been a stoic bunch, not at all prone to elaborate shows of emotion. In a sort of shock-induced trance, I asked my distraught client to follow me down the hall to the office of one of my more experienced colleagues.

Once inside her office, my colleague Becky immediately took control of the situation. She handed the client a tissue and spoke in a soft, soothing voice that calmed both of us down. What dawned on me as I watched Becky comforting my client was: "This must happen every single day at this place. How else could she have handled this flood of tears with such grace and aplomb?" When I asked her about this later that day she confirmed that she had, in fact, dealt with hundreds of client crying jags. And she warned that I needed to prepare myself to do the same. Sure enough, every single day after that, one or more of my clients—both male and female—broke down and sobbed in my office. They wept bitterly and uncontrollably.

The behavior of these tearful clients stood in stark contrast to the behavior of the emotionally numb ones, who were almost entirely without affect and probably had not shed a single tear in years. You might say that the tearful clients were at the opposite end of the emotional spectrum from the majority of our clients, who had virtually succumbed to their drug-induced numbness. In particular, many of the tearful clients felt profoundly unhappy about what they had been putting their families through over the years, and they understandably used their counseling sessions to vent their remorse.

Looked at positively, at least those of our clients who were prone to daily crying jags were still "in touch with their feelings" (albeit excessively so). And the fact that these clients had not shut off their emotions entirely, that they were still capable of expressing rather than suppressing all of their feelings, gave me some reason to hope.

The tearful clients on my caseload were sometimes so sad that they reminded me of Holden Caulfield in J. D. Salinger's *Catcher in the Rye*. Holden worried desperately not only about little children, especially his younger sister, but also about where the Central Park ducks go in winter. Near the end of the story, we learn that his worrying has actually driven him to the brink of insanity. Like Holden, my tearful clients seemed unfit for this cold, cruel world. They were like people born without skin, walking bundles of raw nerve endings. They used drugs to escape from their overwhelming sense of loneliness, and their pain was only further compounded by their belief that no one in the "straight" world cared about them.

"People feel like they can walk all over junkies," they said. "We don't have any feelings, right? So people feel they can spit on us, or kick us when we're down. It doesn't matter because we're sub-human, right? That's what people think of us. But actually, the only time we don't feel is during those couple of minutes when we're 'on the nod.' Outside of that, all we do is feel."

What they wanted more than anything else was love and acceptance. The few tearful clients who had actually been shown genuine affection and tenderness as children just wanted more of the same. And the majority of them, who had not experienced enough parental love, just wanted a little taste of what they had never been given.

Unfortunately, over the course of my year at the clinic, I became somewhat desensitized to all those tears. Compassion fatigue had me firmly in its grip, and as much as it shames me to admit it, I started to feel annoyed by some of the more tearful clients on my caseload. When I confided in my colleagues about this problem, I discovered that they, too, suffered from compassion fatigue. We felt horrible about it, because we had entered a profession that called upon us to act (and feel) humane and compassionate at all times, and yet we were all gradually becoming numb to our clients' anguish.

One of my professors in graduate school specialized in working with sexually and physically traumatized children and adults. In her lectures, she noted that the mere act of revealing all of one's innermost feelings in a "flooding" fashion—as the tearful clients at the clinic were prone to do—is not necessarily a healing experience in and of itself. On the contrary, what my professor referred to as emotional "spilling" can actually re-traumatize clients by forcing them to relive past abuse. In other words, encouraging such vulnerable clients to expose their deepest secrets and fears can sometimes open a "Pandora's box" of new troubles. One of the few times such clients might be urged to "spill" in this manner is when their therapists have a well-thought-out plan about how to contain all those suddenly unleashed emotions.

It was certainly not hard for me to get my tearful clients to open up, since they were always prepared to burst into tears at a moment's notice. My professor further advised that counselors should not allow their egos to be flattered by this sort of "emotional spilling," because such clients are not particularly selective. Tearful clients tend to open up to anyone who is willing to listen to them. When these clients sobbed in my office, it was not because I had worked some therapeutic miracle that had earned me their trust. Rather, it was because they had difficulty controlling themselves and reining in their emotions.

With my clients who cried almost all the time, my greatest challenge became helping them learn how to "contain" their unwieldy emotions. If I did not make emotional containment their number two treatment goal (right after sobriety), what were they supposed to do with all of the old traumas made new again in their therapy sessions? Where were they supposed to "put" all their anguish each week after meeting with me? And finally, how could these exhausting purging sessions strengthen their effort to achieve sobriety?

Emotional containment is vitally important in such cases, because a counselor must enable her clients to feel safe and secure, not only during counseling sessions but also during the long hours in between. If my tearful clients had been better equipped to harness their painful emotions without professional help, they might never have become addicted to heroin in the first place. Many of my clients who wept uncontrollably in my office ended up relapsing on heroin because they found it easier to take drugs than to utilize therapy sessions to "process," or work through, the memories of their past traumas.

In any therapeutic setting, the ultimate goal must always take precedence over everything else. And the ultimate goal of drug counseling is to help clients become and remain drug-free. Dredging up and thoroughly "processing" past traumas may be entirely appropriate in traditional psychoanalysis, but it does not necessarily serve the best interest of all drug-addicted clients. Many opiate addicts have never had the opportunity to develop the emotional capacity or maturity to work through their problems and eventually let them go.

Opiate addicts in emotional crisis are particularly vulnerable to falling back onto their preferred coping mechanism: drug abuse. Unless methadone clients appear to be emotionally stable, their counselors should probably stick to behavior modification techniques (as opposed to intensive psychoanalysis), to avoid triggering a stress-induced relapse.

If clients want to explore a few pertinent past traumas in therapy, then their counselors might consider "following their lead," so to speak. But they should be careful to allow the clients to exercise control over the process, because emotional control is precisely what these clients feel they are lacking. If traumatized persons can gain some sense of control over their painful memories in a safe, quiet setting like their counselor's office, then possibly these memories will no longer have power over them.

The short-term goal of emotional "purging" can be catharsis, but the long-term goal should probably be containment, or moving beyond victimhood to a place of emotional strength. Just because clients have unleashed their emotions, they will not necessarily experience a sense of cathartic release. Do bulimic individuals feel a genuine sense of relief after purging? No. They usually just feel angry and disgusted with themselves. This is often what happened to many of our "purge-prone" methadone clients. They vented and emoted tirelessly in their therapy sessions in the hope of finding peace and relief, but they only ended up feeling spent and over-exposed. An emotional purging is not always the equivalent of a soul cleansing.

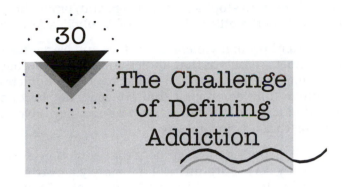

30

The Challenge of Defining Addiction

The definition of an addict is straightforward enough. Simply put, addicts are individuals whose emotional and/or physical dependence on a chemical substance has taken over their lives. But when we try to determine all of the causes and components of this dependence, when we attempt to agree on a definition of addiction that takes into account all of the nuances and complexities of this devastating condition, definitions become more complicated. Anything with the power to rob us of all we hold dear is too strong a force to be easily defined or neatly categorized. As a matter of fact, I would argue that the phenomenon of addiction is mysterious to the point of being sphinx-like.

Nevertheless, we seem to have a strong desire to define addiction in a pat, tidy way. For several decades now (at least since the founding of Alcoholics Anonymous in 1935), the reigning conceptualization of addiction has been that it is a "disease," as opposed to a "moral failing" or a simple matter of will power. The American Medical Association includes the addictive disorders in its roster of mental illnesses, as do the editors of the *DSM-IV*. Certainly, there are physiological components to addiction, and it is also widely accepted in the scientific community that addiction runs in families.

Narcotics Anonymous, an off-shoot of Alcoholics Anonymous, is defined as "a fellowship of men and women who share their experience, strength and hope with each other that they may solve their common problem and help others recover" from substance abuse. In addition, "the only requirement for membership is the desire to stop" abusing drugs and/or alcohol. (These quotes are from the official Web site of Alcoholics Anonymous.)

No matter how many medical doctors and Narcotics Anonymous members maintain that addiction is only a disease, however, it seems that many people—addicts and non-addicts alike—have trouble fully embracing that concept, not because they suspect that it is entirely false, but because they have the nagging feeling that it is incomplete.

I am not disputing the argument that addiction is a disease; it's a perfectly sound argument. I am simply asserting that addiction might also be considered a "disease-plus," a disease not only of the body, but also of the mind and soul. Once a heroin addict physically stabilizes on methadone, he can no longer claim that his body is physically crying out for opiates, because the chemical imbalance in his brain has been corrected.

At that point, he is free to choose sobriety and wellness over a life of ongoing drug abuse. On the other hand, with a clear-cut, purely physiological disease—such as diabetes—free will is a complete non-issue. That is to say, if an insulin-dependent diabetic wants to stay alive, he has no choice about whether or not to inject insulin. On the other hand, if a methadone client truly wants to give up heroin, then (as the commercial says) he must "just do it." It may not seem that simple, but, ultimately, it is.

Again, I am not arguing that we should dispense with the disease model altogether. (I cannot emphasize that enough.) It is an extremely useful tool for conceptualizing an elusive, complex phenomenon—addiction. Yet the disease model is only that: a tool, a frame on which to place more sophisticated ideas. And as a tool or framing device, that is, an abstraction, the disease model should never be assumed to convey the full truth about addiction. Even if one embraces the concept of the disease model, the volitional component of addiction should not be totally overlooked or discounted.

Narcotics Anonymous members argue in one breath that addicts are "powerless" in the face of their addiction, and in the next breath that they have the "power to choose not to use." We all accept that paradoxical contradictions such as this one are at the heart of addiction and recovery. And I believe that it is precisely these layers of complexity that make addiction so much more than just a disease.

We sometimes try to break addiction down into the sum of its parts. I think we do this because, in its gestalt form, the phenomenon of addiction is too overwhelming and unwieldy to be conceptualized in simple terms. As an alternative, I would suggest that we stop trying to define reductively a condition as complex and amorphous as addiction and instead begin to consider the possibility that words alone—especially insufficient, clinical words like "disease"—may never satisfactorily capture all the subtleties and intricacies of such a phenomenon. Perhaps we should not "pathologize" or use medical terminology each and every time we speak of addiction. Something essential, some ineffable dimension of human suffering, gets lost from the discussion when we only look at addiction through a clinical lens.

If we acknowledge the mystery, we can go a long way toward abolishing the reductive mindset that holds that addiction is just a disease, and nothing more. Only then can we make room for multiple points of view in a field that needs multiple points of view. If we can consider alternative definitions of addiction, we might also open our minds to the possibility that different addicts may require different types of treatment.

I am uncomfortable with the contention that addiction is "just a disease" for another reason. "Healing" an addict often seems to be more of an art than a science. The lessons of science can teach us the empirical facts about how and why some people have a biochemical predisposition for addiction. These same facts, however, reveal nothing about an individual addict's personal descent into despair.

In other words, lectures on synapses and dopamine and the interplay of drugs and neurochemistry are fascinating and informative. But scientific analysis is limited to the physiological and sheds little light on existential problems such as human longing or loneliness, which is why I want to include the subject of art in our discussions of science. Unlike scientists, artists make an effort to synthesize rather than dissect the human experience, encouraging us to embrace and celebrate the wholeness, the mystery, and the complexity of our lives. Perhaps, then, we can look to great artists, in addition to great scientists, for a deeper, truer, and richer understanding of addiction. For instance, everyone loves the Impressionist painters because, by distorting visible reality, they uncannily gave us a richer, more resonant version of that reality. By playing with light and color in entirely new ways, they captured the emotional truth of their subjects in a manner that many of the more realistic painters could not.

Aspiring healers (nurses, doctors, psychologists, social workers, and the like) might look to artistic innovators for the inspiration to transform themselves into more intuitive practitioners of the Healing Arts. The Artist reminds the Healer that the true essence of a thing can never be easily or fully known. Consequently, as I have been arguing, the term "disease," while a plausible name for addiction on purely technical grounds, can never adequately convey all there is to know about this enigmatic condition.

Addicts are human beings before they are addicts. Accordingly, they possess the same free will that everyone else possesses. Their free will may be impaired (or buried under layers of anguish), but it is still there as a resource. It's just waiting to be tapped. All addicts have sober, enlightened moments, golden opportunities during which they can make the choice to abstain from drug use. We all have to hold ourselves responsible and accountable for our actions, and this rule applies as much to addicts as it does to anyone else.

Even "dually diagnosed" addicts (that is, addicts who suffer from a severe mental illness, such as paranoid schizophrenia or bipolar disorder, in addition to their addiction) are capable of assuming responsibility for their own behavior, provided they can first stabilize on methadone (and on all the appropriate psychotropic medications).

I know this to be true because as I mentioned earlier, we treated a number of formerly homeless schizophrenic and bipolar addicts who had managed over time to achieve sobriety, obtain appropriate housing, and generally get their lives in order. Not only were these clients taking their psychopharmaceutical medications exactly as prescribed, but they had also managed to take their behavior firmly in hand. And if schizophrenic or bipolar heroin addicts can learn how to modify their behavior in order to achieve sobriety and other life goals, then I believe anyone can.

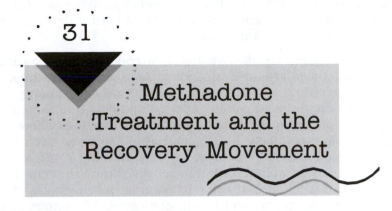

31
Methadone Treatment and the Recovery Movement

As a result of their chronic addiction issues, many recovering heroin addicts find that they do not have fulfilling careers, or happy family lives, or richly satisfying inner lives. They desperately need to fill the hole left by drugs with something else, and Narcotics Anonymous meetings can go a long way toward filling that void.

Not all of our clients cared for self-help meetings. They felt self-conscious because they were in methadone treatment, and some of the recovering heroin addicts they met in meetings had been able to stop using heroin without the aid of methadone. Other clients from our clinic had difficulty with the "war stories" told in these meetings. Addicts tell these stories to remind themselves of just how unmanageable their lives had become during their drug-using days. Our methadone clients who had trouble with the "war stories" claimed that, for them, these tales had the opposite of their intended effect, triggering them to relapse on drugs. Still other clients at our clinic fretted that by going to several meetings a day, they might be letting their other responsibilities fall by the wayside. These clients said they did not want attending meetings to become a "substitute addiction" for them.

Nonetheless, many of our clients found self-help meetings extremely useful, particularly when they were in the early stages of recovery. A Narcotics Anonymous meeting can provide a newly clean and sober individual with a safe place to go, a refuge from the storm. Some clients at the clinic became so enthusiastic about Narcotics Anonymous that they started to chair meetings, and this filled them with a deeply gratifying sense of purpose and pride. Most of all, it can be enormously powerful and comforting for recovering addicts to talk with others who are struggling with the same issues.

Those clients who did not attend Narcotics Anonymous meetings sometimes attended Alcoholics Anonymous meetings instead. According to our clients, some Alcoholics Anonymous chapters are more welcoming of opiate addicts than others, so they "shopped around" until they found AA meetings where they felt safe and comfortable. Unfortunately, some of our clients who chose Alcoholics Anonymous over Narcotics Anonymous had the perception that there was an unspoken hierarchy in the room, with alcoholics at the top, cocaine, marijuana, and pill addicts in the middle, and heroin addicts at the bottom. Thus, even in the theoretically egalitarian setting of a self-help meeting, some of our clients still felt as if they had to battle the same old hatred of heroin users that they had to contend with everywhere else they went. (I am not saying that this is actually the case at AA meetings, only that this was the perception of some of our methadone clients.)

Besides Alcoholics Anonymous, some clients also attended other 12-step groups, such as Overeaters Anonymous, Sex Addicts Anonymous, Gamblers Anonymous, and so forth. Since these clients felt they did everything to excess, they wanted to learn how to practice either moderation or abstinence in virtually every area of their lives.

Some clients said they felt pigeonholed by Narcotics Anonymous, which they claimed made them feel as if they *were* their addictions. So much emphasis is placed on defining oneself as an addict, according to these clients, that other facets of a person's character can sometimes be ignored. People in recovery stand up at self-help meetings and say: "My name is Joe W. I'm an alcoholic, a drug addict, and a compulsive gambler." They introduce themselves this way in order to keep their addictions uppermost in their thoughts at all times. Vigilance, courage, and humility are all essential to achieving and maintaining sobriety. But must addiction always get top billing? By giving his addictions the "leading role" in the documentary film of his own life, is "Joe W." not selling himself a bit short?

Everyone knows that addiction has the power to lay claim to a person's soul. So why elevate it still further? I worry that this elevation, this placing of addiction at the top of the list of one's character traits, may make some recovering addicts feel even more powerless, more enslaved to their "drugs of choice." I am not debating how critical it is for an addict to face his demons. I am saying, rather, that it may not always be entirely beneficial for addicts to identify so completely with their demons.

Rational Recovery, an alternative self-help movement, maintains that addicts are powerful, rather than powerless, that they can literally will themselves out of their predicaments. Rational Recovery was not held in high esteem by most of my colleagues at the clinic, who viewed it as a young, misguided upstart of a self-help program. I do not know what the answers are, but that is exactly the point: no one program has all the answers for every single addict on earth.

At the request of my supervisor, I went to a Narcotics Anonymous meeting. She told me to consider my attending the meeting as a research project, so I walked in with my notebook, prepared to take notes as discreetly as possible. It was a strange and uncomfortable experience; I felt like a spy. Everyone was drinking black coffee and smoking unfiltered cigarettes. People were falling asleep and snoring all around me.

At some point, the man sitting next to me started to tell me his sad life story, and his opening up like that made me feel like an imposter. I decided to "come clean," so I told him I was a drug counselor, that I was not in recovery myself, that I was there as an observer, not a participant. Bits of dried, white spittle clung to the corners of his mouth, and his breath smelled of alcohol, which sort of surprised me. Naïvely, I had assumed that everyone would show up at these meetings sober, if only to support those who were really trying to abstain.

When he learned I was there for "research purposes only," he said: "Honey, you can do all the research you want. But you will never really get it, because you're not inside it. It's like you're on one side of the Grand Canyon and we're on the other. You hear all those stories people are telling? They must sound like they're speaking in a foreign language. You just will not be able to relate, no matter how hard you try."

After my conversation with that man about why I could never fully understand the plight of addicts, I had a greater appreciation of why some methadone clients do not want to be treated by counselors who are not themselves in recovery. Many counselors without drug addiction histories (myself included) lack the patience to deal with the endless relapses. Also, recovering counselors seem to have fewer burnout problems, perhaps because they can still remember being enslaved to their own addictions. All of the recovering counselors I met at the clinic continued to attend self-help meetings on a regular basis, to keep the memories of their own pain and desperation fresh in their minds.

Addicts and non-addicts alike know what it is to crave, because to be human is to crave. Certain philosophies and religions, such as Buddhism, teach the dangers of desire and the great importance of detaching oneself from desire. But my clients informed me that a drug craving is so relentless that it is like no other kind of desire. Because only drug addicts know what it is to experience this unique and excruciatingly painful craving, they can never convey precisely how it feels to non-addicts. Likewise, even if non-addicts have training as counselors, or have a special interest in the struggle of addicts, they can never know the true nature of their clients' suffering from the inside out.

The main quality that non-recovering counselors have to offer their addicted clients is empathy. As I pointed out in my earlier discussion of compassion fatigue, however, a counselor's "empathy well" can sometimes run dry. Recovering counselors, on the other hand, have two wells to draw from: the well of empathy and the well of experience. Not only do some recovering counselors seem more psychologically attuned to their clients, some of them also seem to have a clearer understanding of their erratic behavior.

Even so, some methadone clients prefer to be treated by non-recovering counselors, because they find recovering counselors too strict. Recovering counselors "do not miss a trick," as they say, and their clients know it. These counselors often take a militaristic approach to their work, because they understand exactly how much discipline, vigilance, and structure are required in order for an addict to succeed in treatment. If I had been less of a pushover, if I had modeled my counseling style after that of my recovering colleagues, my clients might have liked me less, but they also might have found our sessions more useful.

The clients who appeared to benefit the most from my soft touch were the ones who had been traumatized or moved from foster home to foster home as children. Because these clients seemed to require a gentle, soothing presence more than anything else, they were very receptive to my counseling style. These clients might have grown into whole, well-adjusted adults if only one teacher or relative had taken a genuine, non-exploitative interest in them during a critical period of their childhood. Unfortunately, instead of being raised under the caring tutelage of supportive mentors, they had grown up in a milieu of neglect and abuse.

After attending that Narcotics Anonymous meeting, I came to understand why some of my clients struggled with the "war stories" of other addicts. It was torturous even for me, a non-addict, to listen to all those people confessing their worst sins to a room full of strangers. As I mentioned earlier, some recovering addicts feel that if they do not share their stories with other addicts on a daily basis, they run the risk of romanticizing their pasts as the "good old days," and setting themselves up for a major fall. Nevertheless, for the uninitiated (such as myself), this barrage of painful memories and self-condemnation felt like an assault on the senses. It was especially upsetting to hear so many people refer to themselves as "lousy, stinking drunks" and "no-good junkies."

I remember one of the speakers in particular, a young woman named Evelyn, who worked as an editorial assistant. She described going home after work to her studio apartment, where her favorite pastimes included listening to opera, reading novels, smoking marijuana, taking Xanax®, and drinking Scotch until she passed out. The music and literature helped her forget her profound loneliness to a certain degree, but the alcohol and drugs obliterated the pain in her heart that was always with her during the daytime when she was busy, but unbearably sober. Evelyn said that as much as she missed the oblivion, she had not succumbed to her urges in five days. But on this night, she could feel the craving taking over. She had come very close to going to the liquor store, but had forced herself to attend this meeting instead. She said she hated meetings, and that she especially hated speaking at meetings, but she had realized that this would be the night she would lose the battle if she did not force herself to speak. Evelyn closed by saying: "I'm nothing, a waste of space, a loser pot-head drunk. I should have been dead a long time ago. I can never forget that."

There was an undeniable power in some of her statements, but they were also worrying. What might she do when she got home? There was extreme self-loathing in her soliloquy. How exactly was Evelyn benefiting from berating herself in public that way? I have trouble believing that this kind of brutal self-flagellation can lead to strong mental health and emotional well-being. True, this shy, bookish woman had briefly emerged from her shell to escape from her loneliness. By the end of her sad monologue, however, she seemed lonelier than ever.

For addicts who desperately want to end their loneliness, going to meetings may suffice. Addicts may find camaraderie and comfort in each other's company. But a self-help group can never take the place of a loving relationship with a significant other, or the consuming passion of a true vocation, nor can it totally dispel an addict's chronic feelings of loneliness and despair.

Leaving that meeting, I kept thinking: there has to be another way. And in point of fact, some of the clients at the clinic had achieved lasting sobriety in alternative ways: by attending religious services rather than self-help meetings, for instance. Such clients maintained that they drew considerably more strength from praying than they did from communing with fellow addicts in self-help meetings.

In the groups that I facilitated at the clinic, people talked about their addictions, but they also talked about other aspects of their lives. Maybe it was inappropriate for me to allow the conversation to stray occasionally from the subject of sobriety. But this was my way of showing my clients that I saw them as more than walking bundles of addiction. And they often told me how much they appreciated these moments in our sessions. "You really see us as human beings. We're not just labels to you," they said.

One of the great strengths of Narcotics Anonymous lies in its ability to provide many axioms or life rules from which recovering addicts might choose. Some of the most successful clients at the clinic viewed the concepts of the recovery movement like the dishes on a buffet table, which allowed them to select certain ideas, while bypassing others. For example, recovering addicts who find solace and courage in the saying "One day at a time" can whisper those words to themselves like a mantra a thousand times a day if that's what they need to do in order to stay clean. In addition, some of the successful clients at the clinic who described themselves as atheists simply bypassed the concept of a "Higher Power" in favor of other Narcotics Anonymous maxims.

On occasion, a client asked me about my own recovery status or lack thereof. I had been advised by some of my more experienced colleagues to "redirect" (read: "deflect") that particular question by saying that this was their treatment, not mine, and that my own status was not relevant to their situation. The majority of my clients, however, never asked me any questions about myself. (I think they assumed that I was too straight-laced to have much of a substance abuse history.) But every once in a while, someone did ask, and invariably I was caught off guard. I would stammer for a while and end up making a clumsy attempt to change the subject, which only succeeded in adding another layer of awkwardness to an already uncomfortable moment.

Once, during a group session, a client suddenly demanded that I disclose my recovery status in front of everyone in the room. Another client, who saw I was fumbling for a reply, leaped to my defense by asserting that my recovery status was neither here nor there. He added that I was a caring counselor, and that this was all that mattered. I was grateful that he spoke up, and touched by what he said.

Later in the session, the client who had demanded to know my status apologized profusely, and he conceded that in the past he had worked with other "non-recovering" counselors who had helped him, and that I had helped him as well. I could not tell if his apology was sincere or if he just felt guilty for having put me on the spot. Either way, I was happy that the "Inquisition" was over.

While not all of our clients utilized Narcotics Anonymous, it certainly was extremely important to many of them. Of course, those who actively participated in Narcotics Anonymous still had to do the extraordinarily difficult work of maintaining their sobriety twenty-four hours a day, seven days a week, on their own. But going to meetings to commune and share their stories with other recovering addicts gave many of them the strength to endure, even during the most trying times.

As much as I felt like a mere observer at the Narcotics Anonymous meeting I attended, and as disturbed as I was by some of the self-disparaging comments made by the speakers, I could still tell that there was something important going on in that room. It had been especially difficult to listen to the young editor, but I have to concede that her testimony was very powerful. There was an undercurrent of energy, a sort of "We can beat this thing together" mentality that made me understand the subtle but undeniable power of unity in sobriety. All of these people had left the quiet and comfort of their homes and trudged through the cold rain to come to this rather uninviting meeting space in order to support one another and themselves in a noble effort, a shared goal. And that alone is a meaningful testament to the importance of the Recovery Movement.

I once asked a recovering alcoholic named Donna what she got out of attending AA meetings. She said: "You know, it's a cold world out there. You walk down the street and no one says hello to you. People wear headphones and listen to music, or they bury their heads in newspapers. They do anything to avoid human contact. Half the time, it seems like no one wants to know anyone else. But when I go to AA meetings, the people I see there look me in the eye and ask me how I'm doing—and they really want to know."

"Do you know most of the people at your meetings?" I inquired.

Donna replied: "It depends. Sometimes I go to meetings where I know there's a good chance I'll run into some of my friends. And it's wonderful. It's like going home. But other times I go to meetings in different towns, just to mix things up a little bit. The amazing thing is that those meetings also feel like home to me. It doesn't matter that I don't know anyone. It only matters that we are all a part of this huge brotherhood. We all have this enormous thing in common, and it unifies us. It makes us a genuine community. People toss that word 'community' around very lightly these days, but that's what AA feels like to me: a very caring and nurturing community. Before AA, I always felt like an outsider looking in on a world that didn't care whether I lived or died. But now I feel like an essential part of the human tapestry."

"It sounds wonderful, that feeling you're describing," I remarked.

"It really is," she said. "I can't think of any other area in my life where I have such a strong sense of solidarity with a large group of people. It's very powerful. I love knowing that when I want a drink so badly I can actually taste the liquor on my lips, I can call my sponsor day or night, and she will drop everything to talk to me. She will make my struggle her top priority for that hour or so, and that's very reassuring to me, very validating. I don't abuse the privilege, but I know that it's there. Truthfully, there are times when I feel very sad and bitter that I have to battle this thing called 'alcoholism' every day of my life. But I try to look at it this way: My alcoholism has given me the opportunity to meet some incredibly loving and supportive people—people I might never have met otherwise. And I can honestly say that I've met some of my favorite human beings in the world at AA meetings."

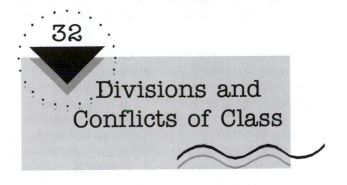

32

Divisions and Conflicts of Class

Drug counselors sometimes say that in families where substance abuse is an issue, drug use is the one topic that no one ever discusses. They refer to this phenomenon as the "white elephant in the middle of the room." I would argue that at methadone clinics, or certainly at the one where I worked, the difference in social class between the clients and the counseling staff was our "white elephant in the middle of the office." The unspoken rule of our work culture was that even in the privacy of our staff meetings, we were not to discuss these differences. By sweeping the thorny subject of class under the rug, we were pretending that we and our clients did not view the world through different sociocultural lenses. Yet no matter how hard we worked at shoring up the pretense that we operated in a workplace free of class divisions, there were times when our collective suburban, middle-class frame of reference seemed to obstruct our mission.

A cross-cultural workshop that I attended in social work school gave me a deeper understanding and appreciation of the different racial and ethnic cultures that make up American society, to prepare me for the work I would be doing with clients from a variety of backgrounds. The facilitator was an African-American woman, while the majority of the workshop participants were white women. One of her messages was that too much time in workplace "diversity training" programs is spent identifying similarities among various subcultures. Her central goal was to remind us that there are also wonderful differences between people of varying racial and ethnic backgrounds—differences that ought to be acknowledged and celebrated. She further contended that we would be significantly better off educating ourselves about these differences instead of pretending they do not exist.

Racially speaking, the clinic was a fairly homogeneous place. Most of the clients and staff members were white. As for variation in socioeconomic class, it was not so much that the staffers had a significantly greater income than the clients, as the fact that we counselors had been granted more opportunities in life than our clients. In addition to having more education, most of the staffers had been exposed to art, culture, and travel in ways the clients had only dreamed about or seen on television. Because of the differences in our backgrounds, we counselors had expectations of life that many of our clients did not have. Some days, the profound unfairness of this fundamental difference hung over all of us like a layer of thick, heavy smog.

These barely acknowledged class differences aggravated the adversarial atmosphere already permeating the culture of the clinic because of the pervasive "counselor-as-law-enforcer" treatment dynamic. Unlike the differences associated with racial or ethnic heritage, class differences do not tend to be something that people tend to "celebrate." People generally feel very proud of their ethnic heritage. But except for those individuals who take a vow of poverty out of religious conviction, or those who live a simple, pared down life in order to make a political statement, very few impoverished Americans feel "proud" of being poor. Quite the contrary. How can one feel "proud" of poverty when virtually all of the external pressures in our society push us to acquire more and more material things and a higher social status?

In countries like Great Britain, where a rigid class system apparently remains deeply entrenched, people may not like the fact that class discrimination exists, but they can at least discuss it openly. In America, by contrast, we prefer to think that we live in a truly egalitarian society, and we go to almost any lengths to avoid discussing class differences.

Nowadays, it is permissible for Americans to talk about such heretofore socially unacceptable topics as sex, politics, and religion, but we are still reluctant to talk about money or class. They remain taboo subjects—subjects that haunt and obsess us but can never be mentioned outside of sociology classes. If an American makes even a neutral remark about social class, he may be viewed as snobbish, uncouth, tactless, or cruel. In fact, the mere acknowledgement of class differences is considered "un-American" in many circles.

Yet, like all "white elephants," the one at the clinic occasionally trumpeted loudly and demanded to be acknowledged. Just how tangled and messy the issue of class can be becomes obvious the instant someone utters a thoughtless, off-the-cuff remark that turns out to be loaded with unwitting assumptions stemming from class affiliation. Class tensions at the clinic were constantly simmering just beneath the surface between the social workers and the clients, as the following vignette illustrates.

Megan, one of the counselors, was having a casual conversation with Tina, a client in the waiting room. Tina mentioned that her young child had recently had a birthday but that she did not have enough money to buy her child a pair of brand-name sneakers for the occasion. Megan suggested to Tina that, instead of shopping at a fancy department store, as she had planned to do, she might instead consider buying a less fancy brand of sneakers at a nearby discount store. It was an innocent suggestion and Megan was clearly trying to be helpful. Unfortunately, however, Tina, feeling patronized, was deeply insulted. She yelled, "Who do you think I am? I shop for my kids at the same places you shop. I'm just like you. How dare you tell me to buy some cut-rate pair of sneakers at some cut-rate store!"

Being poor is very hard to bear. Being urged to be thrifty by someone who is not poor is enraging. All of the class tensions lurking beneath the surface of a seemingly friendly exchange suddenly erupted in an angry lava flow of words. The huge white elephant in the middle of the clinic was trumpeting its head off. In a strange way, the exchange was exciting and cathartic because it was so real. Before that pivotal moment, I had not realized how many of the conversations between clients and counselors had the stiff, semi-formal quality of speakers who keep their guard up in one another's presence at all times.

Megan's suggestion—that Tina consider shopping for a cheaper brand of sneakers at a discount store—was experienced by Tina as a slap in the face for not being able to do right by her child. Megan, of course, had not anticipated how condescending and even accusatory her words would sound to Tina, who had mistakenly inferred that Megan was telling her that she was low-class and unworthy of shopping at an expensive store.

Needless to say, Megan felt terrible for hurting Tina's feelings. She was also furious with herself for not thinking things through before speaking, and for her insensitivity to the question of who was saying what to whom. Precisely because she has so little to offer a child, a drug addict who cannot afford to buy expensive sneakers as a birthday gift should not be discouraged from doing so by someone who obviously can. Even though the entire scenario was rooted in an unfortunate miscommunication, Tina's perception that Megan was patronizing her was as palpably real to Tina as the ground beneath her feet.

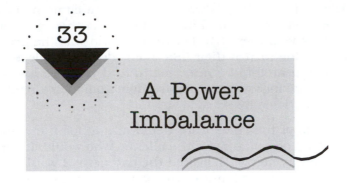

A Power Imbalance

We counselors hated playing the role of "law enforcer" almost as much as the clients hated being treated like criminals. Too often, we felt that we were a "part of the problem rather than a part of the solution." It was especially upsetting when we were required to punish clients we believed to be innocent.

For example, when our clients with physical ailments had trouble providing urine samples on command, we were sometimes asked to rescind their take-home dosing privileges (just as we were to do with clients who consistently refused to provide urine samples). Hearing that their take-home doses were being revoked was particularly devastating for our clients with full-blown AIDS who had earned these privileges. They feared they might not live long enough to regain the take-home doses they had worked so hard to earn. Given how physically weakened and in need of rest they were, the idea of making these clients come into the clinic every single day seemed like a form of cruel and unusual punishment. Several of my colleagues and I were in favor of developing an alternative means of dealing with such clients.

When AIDS first began to decimate the intravenous-drug using population, drug counselors were among the first to sound the alarm and call for more research. Now that a diagnosis of HIV no longer represents an immediate death sentence, it seems that we may have become too blasé about the illness and its devastating implications. Simply because AIDS is now considered relatively commonplace does not mean that its effects are any less life-shattering for its victims.

Many of the HIV-positive clients at the clinic had already lost everything they cared about, including their good health. All that some of them had left in the world was the pride they took in having earned their take-home dosing privileges. Some of them appeared to be near death. And yet here I was, their counselor, taking away one last freedom from their already drastically constricted lives.

If some of the rules were demoralizing for the staff, they were utterly devastating for the clients, who would literally beg us for mercy when we delivered the bad news. I would put myself on auto-pilot and mutter the same old lame excuses about its being a "team decision that was out of my hands." I can hardly blame the clients for being obsessed with the clinic's rigid punishment and reward system, inasmuch as our punitive policies had such an enormous impact on their day-to-day lives.

As I have already pointed out, ours was a "blind-dosing" clinic, because the administration did not want the clients focusing on the number of milligrams in their dosage at the expense of concentrating on their sobriety. But information is another form of power, and whoever possesses it is the one in control. I think that by withholding this information, we staffers may simply have been flexing our muscles, showing the clients "exactly who is boss." I always wondered what harm would have been done if we had told our clients precisely how much methadone they were consuming.

When medical doctors embark on their careers, they take an oath that, above all else, they will do no harm to their patients. I think social workers tacitly take the same oath about their clients. I know that I did not enter the counseling profession in order to punish people who were already extremely deprived. I became a social worker because of my desire to help oppressed individuals regain a sense of hope and find options where they previously believed none existed.

When I worked at the clinic, I often thought back wistfully to the lessons we had learned in graduate school, where we had been instructed to establish and maintain an equal balance of power with our clients. I remember one of my professors saying: "Everyone knows how hard it is to swallow your pride and ask for professional help. Acknowledge this out loud. Commend your clients for their bravery and emotional maturity. Never, ever condescend to them. Most importantly, do everything in your power to create a sense of equilibrium and harmony in the room. Remember that in the end, you and your client are just two human beings sitting in a room and talking."

I tried to keep those words in mind at all times, but I am afraid that in the end I allowed myself to become bogged down in clinic red tape. Ultimately, I yielded to routine and long-standing procedure, permitting the authoritarian culture of the clinic to transform me into just one more bureaucratic representative of "The Man."

34

The Last Straw

Because the clinic had two dosing periods, one in the morning and one in the afternoon, and because so many of the clients coveted the over-crowded morning slot, the administration had devised a system for dealing with this problem. If clients could provide a legitimate-sounding reason for needing an a.m. dose on a given day, they could obtain a "dosing pass" from their counselors that would grant them special permission to dose that morning only. This system was problematic, because clients knew we were too busy to verify the validity of their excuses. As a result, we sometimes ended up giving out too many morning passes, which made for a dangerously chaotic atmosphere around the first-floor dosing window.

Every few months, the nurses would request that the counselors stop issuing morning dosing passes, except in dire—and documented—emergency situations. At times, the overwhelmed dosing nurses would crack down on the counselors, who would in turn crack down on the clients. The whole unhappy situation pitted the downstairs staff against the upstairs staff, and the clients against the counselors, in the process spawning ill will all around. The problematic dosing schedule took its toll on the always fragile client/counselor relationship, by adding yet another source of tension to the strained dynamic already existing between us.

Toward the end of my tenure at the clinic, a dispute with one of my clients over a morning dosing pass almost sent both of us over the edge. One day, at around 10:00 a.m., George approached me outside my office looking particularly frantic. Even on good days, he was a nervous, fidgety person, but on this day, he seemed extra jittery. Something told me not to invite him into my office.

George was an afternoon doser who regularly hounded me for morning passes, and on that morning he wanted yet another pass. His behavior that day was more erratic than usual, and his pupils were the size of pinpoints, which meant that he was probably high. I knew that the nursing staff reserved the right not to dose clients who were visibly intoxicated or extremely agitated. At that moment, George was both. Once again, I explained the overcrowding problem to him, telling him he had to come back later, during his designated dosing slot. In his uninhibited, frenzied state, he kept nagging me for a morning dosing pass.

Luckily, I had the excuse of being on my way to facilitate a therapy group in the clinic's conference room located next to the reception area. When I explained this to him, he did not appreciate being dismissed in this fashion. He followed me, yelling all the while that I was heartless, and that he was entitled to get dosed right that minute. As I slipped into the group room and closed the door behind me, I was unnerved, but I assumed that he would leave the building, and that our last exchange had terminated the episode. A half hour into the group session, however, when I had almost managed to put the incident behind me, I suddenly heard George shouting at the receptionist. I tried my hardest to ignore him, but I could see from the reactions I was getting from my group members that I was not doing a very good job at concealing my apprehension.

Next, I heard one of my colleagues trying to subdue George, who did quiet down eventually. But when the group session ended, there he was, red-faced and simmering right outside the door. As much as I had not wanted to be alone with him before, I did not want to be alone with him now even more. I certainly did not want him to follow me back to my office.

At this point, however, I was more than just afraid; I was angry as well, and ready to stand my ground. I did not raise my voice, but I did tell him that his behavior was completely unacceptable, and that he had to return for his dose in the afternoon as we had discussed earlier. My approach was out of character for me, because usually I avoid confrontations and power struggles. But at that moment, I was convinced that if I did not set clear limits with him right then, he would continue to walk all over me in the future.

That was when he really lost control of himself and resumed his ranting and raving. I ran down the hall to my office, slammed the door behind me, and called security. (So much for my fleeting show of courage.) When the guard came to escort George out of the building, he was still yelling. According to the guard, George waited until I was safely out of earshot to shout: "That f---ing bitch! If she was a guy, I would have blindsided her. That's what I should have done. I should have sucker-punched her sorry ass when she wasn't looking!"

Even though I did not hear George utter these words with my own ears, when the guard later told me what he had said, I panicked. I do not know whether this disturbing event was a breaking point, or a turning point, but it was definitely an ending point. When the administrators learned what had happened, they suggested I go home early; I was more than happy to take them up on their offer. Some of my colleagues could see that I was upset, so they escorted me all the way to the train station. Believe it or not, we had to walk right past George, who was sitting on a park bench in front of the clinic. When he saw me walking by, he gave me a dirty look. Thankfully, however, he remained calm and did not say a word.

I boarded the train, and as we pulled out of the station, I wondered if I would ever return to the clinic, or if I would just call in "sick" for the rest of my life. On my trip home, it dawned on me that I had chosen exactly the wrong moment to teach George a lesson about not behaving like a bully. My own bottled up frustration had at last gotten the better of me. (In retrospect, I sometimes ask myself if I allowed the situation to escalate to the point where I would finally have a good enough excuse to quit.)

Regardless of George's bad behavior, I did not have to surrender to my own anger to show him that I had the upper hand. I had permitted myself to do something I had never wanted to do, to get caught up in a childish power play with a client. In the process, I had forgotten everything my teachers had taught me about the importance of shifting the balance of power in my clients' favor. The open hostility George had exhibited had confirmed my worst fears about any client's potential for violence.

But that was not enough to justify my giving into and embracing the authoritarian ethos of the clinic. When I began working there, my dream had been to uphold the egalitarian tenets of the social work profession by serving my clients, rather than subjugating them. Somewhere along the way I had done the unthinkable: I had lost sight of my dream, sacrificed my values, and given in to the overly punitive mores of my work culture.

When I returned to the clinic a few days after the unnerving incident, I think that everyone on the staff could probably tell that my days there were numbered. If the clients had heard anything about what had transpired, they did not mention it to me or treat me any differently. At my request, George was removed from my caseload. When I told my family and friends about my decision to quit, they were happy to see me leaving in one piece, which makes me think I should be grateful to George for providing me with an escape hatch.

35

Tragedy at the Clinic

One day, shortly after the confrontation with George, by which time I had already decided to resign but had not yet given my notice, Jane, a support staff person at the clinic, received terrible news. Though I did not know Jane very well, she had always been a friendly presence in the building. When she got word that her adult daughter—an active drug addict—had been murdered as part of a drug-related crime spree, at first no one at the clinic could believe that it was true.

Only an hour before she heard the news, Jane and I had been talking and laughing in the elevator. I can remember complimenting her on her outfit, a beige blouse and a matching skirt. I remember that she was excited about the jewelry she had selected to go with the outfit: a pretty beaded necklace that she had made herself. I know now that I will never forget either that outfit or that necklace, because a short time later Jane would be the recipient of the kind of catastrophic news that only happens to other people, not to anyone we know, or so we tell ourselves.

Even the way she heard the news was horrifying. The state police called when they were still an hour away from the office. When she burst into tears and pleaded with them to tell her what was going on, they said they were not at liberty to discuss what had happened on the telephone. As soon as they said that, Jane knew in her heart that something terrible had happened to her daughter, who had been struggling with drug abuse on and off for more than ten years. She said later that even though she had always feared her daughter might meet a tragic end, until that very moment, she had somehow managed to hang onto hope.

Prior to that terrible day, Jane had occasionally received messages on her answering machine from malicious prank callers claiming that her daughter had overdosed. She knew right away that this was no prank call. Also, in her nightmares, she had received such calls. In her dreams, however, the call always came in the middle of the night, whereas in real life, the police had reached her at her workplace. They had then made her wait a full hour just to hear the terrible words she already knew were going to be spoken. The pain that the family members of drug addicts go through every day is as inconceivable as it is commonplace. Mothers and fathers of addicts are regularly asked to go to city morgues to identify the swollen, virtually unrecognizable corpses of their children, who have either overdosed or been murdered.

I did not see Jane leave the building after talking to the police. I did not bear witness to the look of devastation on her face, as some of my colleagues did. But I knew she was shattered. In the morning she'd been whole; in the afternoon, she was broken into a thousand pieces. That's how quickly and irrevocably one's life can be changed by a single phone call. The haunting expression that some of my colleagues observed on her face as she departed was the ghost-white mask of death. Part of her had perished along with her daughter. Ever since that day I have tried to imagine what it would be like to hear that one of my loved ones had been murdered, but I simply cannot.

I was amazed at how quickly Jane returned to work after the funeral. The next time I bumped into her in the elevator (our usual meeting place), I said: "Jane, I'm so sorry. How are you doing?"

She replied, "Not great. But I had to come back to work. I was going crazy at home. As long as I have things to do, I can distract myself for a while. That's why it's better to be in the office. It's when I don't have anything to do that I start thinking about everything, and that's when I really get myself into trouble."

"That sounds like a good idea—coming back to work," I offered.

"Well," she said, "I'm not going to pretend there aren't moments when I don't want to curl up in a ball and die. But I can't. There are too many people counting on me: my grandson, my husband, my mother. They all give me a reason to get up in the morning. Without them, I just don't know what I would do."

"It sounds like you're giving each other a lot of strength and support," I said.

"I know. But I've been looking for some outside support as well. In fact, I've been leaving phone messages at this organization that sponsors bereavement groups for the family members of homicide victims. The thing is, they never call me back. And I have yet to get a 'live person' on the other end of the phone when I call there."

"That's terrible. I wonder what's going on."

"I have no idea. But let me tell you, the silence has been deafening. It really makes the pain of losing her a lot worse. Here I am, reaching out for support, just like everyone has been telling me to do, but I can't get a hold of the very people who could help me the most. They are the only ones who can completely understand what I've been going through, and yet they're totally unreachable."

Jane added that on the positive side, she had been able to take some comfort in the resilience and abiding spirituality of her grandson (the five-year-old son of her slain daughter), who said: "Now that Mommy's with God, she can go to Disney World whenever she feels like it." She was continually amazed at the little boy's grasp of the permanence of the loss. Because of her daughter's drug problem, Jane had had custody of her grandson for most of his young life, and his contact with his mother had been limited. Now Jane was hoping that this limited contact would help him heal quickly.

Jane's sorrow and frustration fed into the sadness and anger I was already feeling because of my confrontation with George. It had an equally devastating effect on nearly everyone who worked at the clinic. The clients were not informed of the tragedy, but I'm sure they could tell by the looks on our faces that something was terribly wrong.

Because the administrators could tell that the event and its aftermath were having a very negative impact on staff morale, they eventually decided it was necessary for the counselors to "process" our feelings about the murder at one of our team meetings. (Jane was not present at this meeting.)

Initially, the discussion was painful and awkward. None of us knew quite what to say. But after a long silence, one of my wise colleagues said a few words that were difficult to hear, but resonated with all of us. She pointed out that not only was the murder a tragedy for Jane and her family, but it was also hard for us to accept, partly because it was drug-related, and partly because it struck too close to home. As terrible as this may sound, we had come to expect a few tragedies of this sort to befall some of our clients every year, because of the dangerous lives they led. But we had never expected anything like this to happen to the family member of a co-worker. She was on "our side." An invisible dividing line had been crossed, and we felt overwhelmed and violated. We had always kept our clients' suffering at arm's length, saying that we needed to maintain our professional distance. I now suspect that the deeper reason we were so intent on keeping our clients' problems at bay was our unspoken fear that if we got too close, we might be "infected" by their anguish. We were deathly afraid that if we did not erect a wall around ourselves and call it "clinical distance," the clients would "invade our territory" and bring all of their pain and suffering with them.

Now that the clients' world had collided so tragically with ours in the form of murder, we were forced to confront the fact that all of us were vulnerable to the whims of a cruel, randomly destructive world. The murder of Jane's daughter brought to light the painful truth that we could no longer seek refuge in our flimsy "us-versus-them" fantasy. Our delusion that the clients were different from us in some inexpressible but crucial way had finally been forever destroyed by something as obvious and yet as difficult to face as our common mortality.

36

"Forgiveness Artists"

A t a substance abuse conference, I had a conversation with a social worker named Karen, who was working with children with AIDS and their families. Karen talked about working with a very ill, HIV-positive four-year-old boy, Evan. Evan made me think of my co-worker Jane's grandson, who was also being raised by his maternal grandmother. Evan's mother was too strung out on crack and heroin to care for him herself.

Once Karen had asked Evan if he ever felt angry at his mother, hoping to provide him with the opportunity to vent the rage Karen was sure had to be bottled up inside. After all, his mother was never around. Also, she had infected him with the AIDS virus. Evan stunned Karen and moved her to tears when he replied, "Why should I be mad at my Mommy? Just because I'm sick? It's not her fault."

Karen said: "Technically, of course, it was his mother's fault that he was sick. But Evan didn't care about that. He simply wasn't interested in pinning the blame on anybody, least of all his mother."

I was as humbled as Karen was, not so much by Evan's devotion to his mother—most children feel that way—but by his boundless, unflinching sense of forgiveness, his generosity of spirit in the face of his own devastating illness. "You have to understand," Karen explained, "that it had reached the point where Evan was so sick he could barely go outside to play with his friends. Yet for some mysterious reason, he was capable of this astonishing degree of forgiveness."

Evan clearly loved his mother unconditionally, and he was unfazed by the fact that she was unable to take care of him herself. Karen also remarked, "Evan sometimes seemed melancholy, but he didn't appear to have a bitter or resentful bone in his entire body."

Forgiveness like that strikes me as nothing short of miraculous. I noticed that among my clients who were able to attain sobriety, many of them shared Evan's generosity of spirit. Like him, they were able to forget about old grudges and let bygones be bygones. Forgiveness gave them the strength not to succumb to their anger and fear.

Unlike most of my clients, I have been fortunate enough to have known several inspiring mentors in my life—mentors who remind me in spirit of young Evan. For instance, many years ago, my now deceased writing teacher was run over by a car shortly after stepping out of his own car to assist another driver who had pulled over onto the shoulder of the road with engine trouble. After many painful operations, he ended up losing one of his legs and the use of the other. Although confined to a wheelchair, he never lost his generous spirit, nor did he lose his desire to teach, which he continued to do at his home for the rest of his life. What most impressed me about him is that, through prayer and writing and teaching, he had found it in his heart to forgive the woman who had accidentally run him over. His enormous capacity for forgiveness—along with his other wonderful qualities—made him a cherished role model for me. Now that he is gone, he is desperately missed by all of us who viewed him as a guiding light.

Another mentor was one of my social work professors. He had spent the first half of his social work career working in prisons, and he once told us about a client who had smashed his baby's head against the wall to stop the child from crying, killing the infant instantaneously. My professor firmly believed that to be an effective counselor, he had to place himself in the shoes of all of his clients, even the ones who had committed murder. At the time, he was himself the father of young children and he understood how their constant crying might drive a person mad. His soul-searching permitted him to see that his client was not a monster; he was only a man who had succumbed to the same monstrous impulses we all possess but are generally able to control. My professor was able to "separate the sin from the sinner," not by taking the self-righteous, morally superior position that he was somehow better than or different from his clients, but by coming to grips with the fact that under the right conditions he might be just as capable as a convicted killer of committing a capital crime.

My professor showed us that if we wanted to become truly effective social workers, we would have to acknowledge our own fallibility as human beings. Only then would we be able to open our hearts fully to our clients. It was evident from the way in which he told the story that his realization had been an epiphany for him, and it had marked an important breakthrough for him not only as a therapist but also in his personal evolution as a deeply spiritual and humane man.

When I consider the innate goodness of some of the "forgiveness artists" I have been lucky enough to know and hear about, I realize that they all have something to teach us about how to live with dignity and compassion. Karen told me that young Evan later died. But in the short time he was here, he taught those of us who heard his story a great deal about how to live in the world. Perhaps as children we all know how to forgive as Evan did, completely and non-judgmentally. And perhaps when we become adults, learning the art of forgiveness may only be a matter of "remembering" what we already know in our hearts.

37

A New Vision of Treatment

I had a colleague who used to say: "One day, we'll look back on methadone clinics and we'll think: *My God. What a barbaric form of treatment.*" I hope he is right.

For clients who are highly motivated to succeed, methadone treatment can be extremely effective. The current treatment model is considerably less effective, however, for clients who have neither "hit rock bottom" nor experienced epiphanies that would provide them with the necessary incentive to become and remain drug-free. After all, an addict's desire and motivation to break free from the chains of addiction must come from within. I believe, however, that the current treatment model could and should be substantially modified so as to better serve the needs of all opiate-addicted clients, not only the most motivated among them.

My colleagues who had been in the field for years informed me that approximately eight out of ten clients who complete a course of methadone treatment end up relapsing on heroin and other drugs. This heartbreaking statistic tells us that we would be fools not to think about revamping the entire system. Methadone clients are well aware of depressing facts like this one, and their awareness makes them afraid to leave treatment. Their fear immobilizes them, enslaving them to the very system that is supposed to be helping them, freeing them.

A methadone clinic, I discovered, is so much more than a place. It is also a state of mind, which is why it can be so hard to leave behind. Furthermore, at least half the clients at the clinic continued to abuse illegal drugs while on methadone. Going to the clinic was especially unsettling for clients who were genuinely trying to stay clean, because they were forced to run the gauntlet of dealers waving drugs in their faces whenever they entered or left the clinic.

Considering the problems of the current treatment system, I would like to propose a new treatment model. My proposal is fairly radical, in that it would eventually eliminate the need for methadone and methadone clinics. I believe that the system outlined in this chapter would be both more effective as a remedy and less stigmatizing as an experience for clients. In addition to benefiting opiate addicts, it would satisfy the demands and the needs of politicians, businesspeople, service providers, community activists, and the public at large.

I would suggest, first of all, that methadone, over a period of time, be replaced throughout the country by a similar but longer-acting opiate replacement drug called levo-alpha-acetyl-methadol, or LAAM, which I discussed briefly in Chapter 3. LAAM has already been FDA-approved for use, and is now available as a viable alternative to methadone treatment at a limited number of facilities. Switching from methadone to LAAM, therefore, would involve none of the start-up costs associated with the research and development of a new pharmaceutical. When I say that LAAM is "longer-acting" than methadone, I mean that a dose of LAAM metabolizes slowly in the client's system over the course of several days, unlike a dose of methadone, which is effective for only twenty-four to thirty-six hours. In fact, clients need to take LAAM only three times a week.

The appeal of an agent like LAAM is that since it lasts so much longer than methadone, it eliminates the need for take-home dosing. More significantly, it also eliminates the game-playing and power struggles between client and counselor that can accompany take-home dosing. I am certain that this reform would go a long way toward abolishing the punitive "carrot-and-stick" disciplinary protocol now in operation at so many methadone clinics.

In addition, since clients would not have the opportunity to carry their LAAM doses on their person (the doses would be administered in a doctor's office), at one fell swoop the illegal sale by clients of their take-home doses would be halted. Methadone advocates argue that methadone cuts down on heroin-related crime, and this may be true. From what I observed in my year at a methadone clinic, however, a whole new crime culture blossoms around methadone clinics, a culture founded upon the illegal sale of take-home doses, urine samples, pills, cocaine, marijuana and, of course, heroin. But it should come as no surprise that drug dealers flock to the areas around methadone clinics; they understand only too well that they have a built-in customer base in these neighborhoods.

Methadone clinics often serve as centralized locations for addicts to get together to deal drugs, get high, turn tricks, buy and sell take-home doses and clean urine samples, and the like. As I have already pointed out, methadone clients are nothing if not entrepreneurial. Clearly, not all methadone clients stop engaging in addictive and criminal behavior just because they are in treatment, in part because they trigger one another to continue abusing drugs. In addition, some clients pick up more drug habits at methadone clinics than they had before entering treatment. I have often wondered what the policymakers who created methadone clinics could have been thinking when they decided to assemble hundreds of addicts in one centralized location.

Neighborhood merchants resent the presence of clinics, because they worry that clients will shoplift and also scare away paying customers. Knowing how some methadone clients behave, I can hardly blame merchants for harboring such fears. Moreover, several prominent politicians have in recent times announced publicly their strong anti-methadone position, and have rallied community support for their position. Not long ago, when I asked a fervent methadone advocate if she would like a methadone clinic to open in her own neighborhood, she confessed that she would not. Another former colleague was instrumental in overturning a proposal to open a methadone clinic in his community because he knew that, among other things, it would drive down property values. If those of us who work in the field do not want clinics opened in our neighborhoods, how can we justify asking others to welcome methadone clinics into theirs?

As I envision it, a huge part of the solution lies in keeping the clients apart from one another. There is only one sure way to achieve this, one way to continue dispensing an opiate replacement medication to the clients who need it without allowing them all to congregate in the same place day in and day out.

Here is the plan:

First, as I already indicated, I would suggest replacing methadone with LAAM. This would have to be done gradually, in a controlled and careful format. Secondly, I would recommend recruiting physicians involved in research and/or in private practice and affiliated with reputable hospitals or other medical institutions, who are also humane and knowledgeable about the cunning ways of substance abusers. These physicians must be willing to have a handful of addicts dose in their private offices on a regular basis. If clients were to "scatter dose" throughout the city, they would not be compelled to gather in one centralized location. This arrangement would surely curtail drug dealing among clients, not to mention its potential for reducing the "triggering" effects of putting active addicts together with other active addicts.

If opiate addicts were able to dose discreetly in the privacy of their doctor's offices, instead of at a site widely known as a clinic for drug addicts, they would feel far less stigmatized in their communities. All the talk about "client confidentiality" notwithstanding, in point of fact when clients receive drug treatment at a known methadone clinic, all who frequent the area—residents, police, local merchants—quickly brand them "junkies" and come to regard them with deep suspicion.

Regarding the matter of client confidentiality, I occasionally noticed reporters and cameramen from some of the local news stations filming clients as they entered the clinic. I do not know if any of this footage was ever broadcast, but I do know that the clients who were filmed were extremely agitated and distraught at the thought of what could happen to them if it was. They were terrified that their family members and employers might learn they were in drug treatment and either disown them or fire them from their jobs. If clients could go to their doctor's private office for LAAM dosing, then they would never have to worry about cameramen, merchants, police, other addicts, or anyone else who might figure out that they were in drug treatment.

As for drug counseling, my considered opinion is that it should not be a mandatory part of treatment. Clients (like most of us) generally respond negatively when ordered to do something. If the counseling component of the program were made voluntary, I am convinced that many clients would have a more positive attitude about it. They could receive their counseling on their own volition at mental health clinics located all over town, rather than at one central location. They could start and stop going to counseling at will. In this way, drug counselors could function purely as therapists, rather than as law enforcers.

I am further convinced that counselors should not be asked to discipline their clients. Client discipline should be the exclusive domain of the program administrators, who would also be charged with monitoring the urinalysis component of treatment. Not only do therapists have no training as police, most have little or no interest in functioning as both counselor and "law enforcer." And if there is one thing we need in the substance abuse field, it is greater clarity about the counselor's role in treatment. Forcing counselors to double as disciplinarians erodes client trust. If counselors could concentrate exclusively on helping clients modify their negative thinking and self-destructive behavior, I am convinced that more clients would make better progress in treatment.

The counselors and doctors who agree to participate in the LAAM drug treatment program should make sure they have diversified caseloads. In other words, they should never agree to take on more than four or five opiate-addicted clients at a time. Heroin addicts can be extremely draining to treat, so they should never comprise a counselor's entire caseload. A cap on the number of opiate-addicted clients would allow counselors to work with a wider range of clients. It would thus help reduce counselor burnout. And burnout, along with the related problem of rapid counselor turnover, is a major problem in the field of drug counseling.

To recap briefly, the following list is a more succinct version of the reforms set forth in greater detail above:

1. **Replace methadone with longer-acting LAAM**, which is already in use at some facilities. Because LAAM already exists, there would be no research and development costs associated with its more widespread use. This reform would eventually eradicate the need for a take-home dosing system and all the attendant problems, such as illicit methadone dealing, and counselor/client power struggles over take-home dosing privileges.

2. **Decentralize treatment** to provide more discreet care and to destigmatize clients by gradually abolishing methadone clinics in favor of a "scattered site" treatment model that utilizes pre-existing doctors' offices, hospitals, and mental health facilities in various locations.

3. **Recruit and train** only those physicians and mental health professionals with proven track records in the substance abuse treatment field, those who already have a solid understanding of the special needs and behaviors—including the criminal tendencies—of some opiate addicts.

4. **Place strict limits** on the number of opiate addicts on any given doctor's or counselor's caseload, capping the amount at four or five per practitioner. This reform would minimize staff burnout and consequent turnover, and maximize the amount of individual attention received by each client.

5. **Establish a separate administrative body** that would serve as the disciplinary "arm" of the treatment protocol, handling all client disturbances and behavioral problems. Such a body would allow participating doctors and counselors to function exclusively as care providers, rather than as law enforcement officers, paving the way for increased client trust and decreased client confusion over counselor "role-blurring." The administrative branch would also be responsible for all aspects and phases of the clients' urinalysis.

6. **I would recommend a very slow transition from methadone treatment to LAAM treatment, as clients and service providers alike would need time to adjust.** It goes without saying that further details in this reform plan would have to be worked out during the implementation phase. Empirical studies would need to be conducted, and pilot programs carried out. New information could then be disseminated to participating care providers, identifying current problems and new solutions. Also, a very clearly defined referral procedure would have to be established between medical and counseling practitioners and the administrative body, since disciplinary problems would have to be turned over to the administration as quickly as possible. Beyond the recruitment of qualified, committed personnel, only those medical and mental health facilities which are deemed "LAAM-friendly" would be selected as participating treatment sites.

Funding for this alternative program should not be too difficult to obtain, inasmuch as the whole idea of using a "scattered
site" model would be to utilize only those facilities, resources,
and personnel that are already in place. The only funds that
would have to be raised, or perhaps simply reallocated, would
be for staff training and the creation of a separate administrative branch of the program.

Many politicians vociferously object to methadone treatment.
In certain respects, they are right in doing so. In my view, it
would be best if everyone began to think in terms of gradually
closing the doors of methadone clinics. Of course, we should
not abolish methadone treatment without first establishing an
alternative treatment model, such as the one outlined above. I
cannot emphasize this point enough. It would be inhumane to
leave clients without treatment. In addition, crime rates would
likely increase substantially, because addicts would resume using
heroin, once again being forced by the painful nature of their
opiate addiction to deal and steal. As counselors, we often ask
our clients to make monumental changes in their behavior. Therefore, we must also be willing to reform the current treatment
system in order to help our clients make the difficult changes
we expect of them.

Living the life of a typical heroin addict is punishment enough.
Politicians should worry less about penalizing addicts, and more
about offering them a helping hand. One of the problems faced
by addicts is that they have no identifiable political lobby working on their behalf. Politicians have little time or patience for
constituents who fail to make their presence known through
the ballot box. Traditionally, drug addicts tend not to vote in
great numbers. Because end-stage heroin addicts tend to be
both apolitical and powerless, politicians either overlook them
or see them as merely worthless criminals, a blight on society.
These same politicians would do well to shift their focus away
from struggling street addicts to the real criminals, the big-time
dealers who are more than happy to feed the addicts' need for
illicit drugs.

We must remember that addicts start out life like everyone
else. For a variety of reasons, some of which may be unknow-
able, when they can no longer bear the burden of living their
lives with the cards fate has dealt them, they use drugs to kill
their feelings and escape their emotional pain. Addiction casu-

alties are all around us. The ravaged souls in our midst are piled so high I am sometimes amazed we do not trip over them. It shames me to admit that during the year I worked at the clinic, my own compassion waned as my frustration increased. Now that I have stepped back and regained at least some of my former perspective on life, I only ask that our elected politicians try to do the same. It comes down to a question of basic human rights: addicts are human beings, and therefore inherently deserving of humane treatment.

The desire for unconditional love and acceptance is something we all share. But when that desire is thwarted, darkness beckons, often in the guise of drugs. Freud, inspired by the ancient Greeks, speculated that Eros is locked in perpetual battle with Thanatos, fighting for domination of the human psyche. He asserted that the two opposed instincts burn deep inside each one of us, the impulse toward love and life (Eros) and the drive toward annihilation and death (Thanatos). Freud also believed that it is the tension born of this great war that gives our lives meaning. When Thanatos wins out—as he does with so many drug addicts—living becomes a state of chronic numbness and nihilistic oblivion, a sort of death in life. My methadone clients taught me the true meaning of despair. But they also taught me that it only takes a tiny spark of hope to reignite the flame of the human spirit. And where there is even the smallest glimmer of hope, Eros (love)—life—can never be far behind.

Glossary of Terms

Abscess—an infection or localized wound surrounded by inflamed tissue that may be caused by excessive intramuscular drug use.

Addiction—a compulsive need for and use of a habit-forming drug, such as heroin or cocaine. Sometimes refers to other compulsive behaviors.

ADHD, or Attention Deficit Hyperactivity Disorder—a disorder characterized by inattention, impulsivity, and hyperactivity.

AIDS—acquired immune deficiency syndrome; the end stage of HIV disease, which is caused by HIV, or the Human Immunodeficiency Virus.

Alcoholics Anonymous (AA) or Narcotics Anonymous (NA)—well-organized support groups for alcoholics and/or addicts who desire lasting sobriety.

Antisocial Personality Disorder—a personality disorder characterized by such symptoms as aggressiveness, indifference to the safety of others, a tendency to fight frequently, deceitfulness, impulsivity, and a lack of remorse.

Arrested Development—stopped or delayed emotional growth, often observed in drug addicts, who sometimes seem to stunt their maturation process by abusing drugs.

Axis II Disorders—a clinical category that includes personality disorders, such as Narcissistic Personality Disorder and Borderline Personality Disorder, and mental retardation.

Benzodiazapines or Benzos—anti-anxiety pills administered to individuals who suffer from genuine anxiety disorders, but frequently abused by drug addicts.

Bipolar Disorder—a severe mental illness often characterized by an alternating cycle of manic and depressive episodes.

Black Tar Heroin—a very potent and inexpensive dark-brown form of heroin that enters the United States via Mexico and is used primarily in southern and western states like Texas and California and has been associated with a high number of deaths.

Blind-Dosing—an administrative policy not to disclose to clients the amount of methadone they are ingesting.

Blocking Dose—a dose of methadone that is high enough to prevent clients from feeling intoxicated if they use heroin, but not so high that they feel intoxicated from the methadone.

Booting—a slang term for injecting a small amount of heroin into the vein, then pulling some blood back into the syringe, injecting a little more of this mixed liquid, and so on. This practice induces a series of small bursts of euphoria.

Borderline Personality Disorder—an Axis II disorder, the symptoms of which include the formation of intense, short-lived relationships, self-mutilating behavior, displays of rage, chronic feelings of emptiness, and an unstable or shaky sense of self.

The Chase—the relentless cycle of illegal activities, such as prostitution, dealing, and stealing, that addicts feel compelled to engage in to obtain enough illegal drugs to avoid going into withdrawal.

Cheeking—a slang expression for holding methadone in one's mouth with the express purpose of depositing the methadone into another person's mouth in exchange for money.

Chipping—a methadone client's continued use of small amounts of heroin to supplement the methadone in his system.

Client Confidentiality—the right of clients to have their treatment kept private.

Clinician—a practitioner (rather than an academic, a researcher, an administrator, or a policy maker) who is qualified and licensed in the clinical practice of medicine, psychology, mental health care, or social work.

Cognitive-Behavioral Treatment—a form of psychotherapy that focuses on a client's ability to identify and alter destructive patterns of thought and behavior.

Cognitive or Emotional Dissonance—a feeling of malaise based on the sense that one's emotional or cognitive experience is in conflict with one's beliefs or worldview.

Compassion Fatigue—the numbness and emotional exhaustion and depletion that counselors often feel after treating excessive numbers of traumatized clients.

Compliant Clients—clients in a methadone treatment program who follow clinic rules and who also become fully engaged in their therapy.

Cooking—the process of heating and dissolving heroin mixed with liquid in preparation for injection.

Cotton Fever—a feeling of severe nausea and other agonizing symptoms brought on by using heroin that has been cut with a toxic substance.

Countertransference—the vast range of feelings that clients inspire in their counselors.

Corrective Emotional Experience—a therapist's effort to forge a healthy client/counselor bond in order to compensate for a client's past emotional traumas, the ultimate goal of which is to equip the client with the emotional tools needed to form healthy relationships.

Cutting—diluting a drug supply by blending it with other substances to decrease the drug's potency and to increase profitability for dealers.

Dealer—a person who sells or distributes illicit drugs to addicts and other drug users.

Detoxify—to stop using a toxic or addictive narcotic substance, such as heroin, and/or to free oneself from continued dependence on such substances.

Dope—slang for heroin and other drugs.

Dope-Sick—slang for being in a painful state of withdrawal from heroin.

Dosing Pass—a signed permission slip that allows a methadone client to dose at a time other than his usual dosing time.

Drug Culture—a subculture comprised of individuals who use or abuse illicit drugs, engage in criminal activities to support their drug habits, interact mainly with one another, and make extensive use of drug-related terminology.

Drug of Choice—an addict's preferred illicit or licit substance.

DSM-IV—a comprehensive reference book used by mental health professionals, which contains a descriptive listing of all psychological disorders organized into five clinical or diagnostic categories known as "axes."

Empathy—the ability of one person to identify strongly with the feelings of another and to offer support based on that profound sense of identification.

Enabling—a term used in the Recovery Movement to describe friends and family members of addicts who aid and abet these addicts by providing them with money, a rent-free residence, and/or other gifts despite the addicts' continued drug abuse.

Epiphany—in the context of substance abuse treatment, a stunning revelation that one has reached the point when it is necessary to stop using drugs forever or face possible death.

Eros—the ancient Greek god of love and life.

Getting Over—a slang expression for lying to or deceiving authority figures.

Going Straight—slang for abstaining from drugs and exiting the drug culture.

Group Therapy—psychological counseling for a group of clients who are tackling a common problem, such as substance abuse.

Harm Reduction Treatment Model—a model of methadone treatment based on the idea that it is an adequate treatment outcome for methadone clients to achieve some (as opposed to all) of their treatment goals.

Hepatitis—a family of viral diseases that attack the liver and cause multiple other health problems.

High—a drug-induced feeling of intoxication, euphoria, or peace.

Hitting Bottom—slang for reaching the point when one must stop using drugs forever or face possible death.

HIV—Human Immunodeficiency Virus, the virus that causes AIDS and attacks the immune system, rendering the body vulnerable to many life-threatening illnesses.

Hustling—also known as "scamming," slang terms for participating in deceptive and/or criminal activities in order to acquire money for drugs.

Individual Therapy—psychological counseling for an individual client.

Intramuscular Drug Use—also known as "Skin-Popping"—injecting heroin directly into the muscle of the upper arm or thigh rather than injecting it into the vein.

Involuntary Detoxification—the very rapid lowering of a non-compliant client's methadone dosage, against the client's wishes.

Junkie—a derogatory slang term for a heroin addict.

LAAM, or Levo-Alpha-Acetyl-Methadol—a synthetic opiate similar to methadone that prevents the emotional highs and lows associated with heroin abuse by blocking the neural receptors that process heroin. Unlike methadone, LAAM metabolizes slowly.

Liquid Handcuffs—a slang term used by methadone clients to describe their feeling of being enslaved to the methadone clinic.

The Man—a derogatory term for "The Establishment" or for authority figures who represent "The Establishment," such as the police.

Mandatory Counseling—the practice of compulsory psychotherapy, often used in conjunction with pharmacological treatment.

Mentoring—providing guidance, tutelage, support, and encouragement to a child, teenager, or adult.

Methadone Client—an individual who receives outpatient psychotherapy combined with pharmacological treatment in the form of methadone, a synthetic opiate.

Methadonia—a tongue-in-cheek term coined by methadone clients to describe a methadone clinic; conveys the idea that the clinic is more than just a physical place. It is also a "country of the mind."

Morphine—an addictive drug derived from opium and used (like all opiates) to alleviate pain and induce sleep.

Narcissistic Personality Disorder—an Axis II disorder characterized by grandiosity, a sense of entitlement, a lack of empathy, a sense of self-importance, a need for constant admiration, and a tendency to exploit others. Narcissists are believed to suffer from a deep psychic "wound" that compels them to develop a virtually impenetrable emotional defense system.

Narcotics Anonymous—a well-organized support group for narcotic addicts.

The Needle—slang term for the syringes addicts use to inject heroin and other drugs.

Nodding Out or Being On the Nod—slang for entering a semiconscious state after the initial rush of euphoria that occurs immediately following the injection of heroin.

Opiate Replacement Therapy—treatment of drug addicts that involves the substitution of a man-made opiate (LAAM or methadone) in the heroin addict's system.

Opiates—narcotic substances derived from poppies, such as morphine or heroin. There are also man-made opiates, such as methadone and LAAM.

Outpatient—a client who receives treatment at a hospital, agency, or clinic without staying overnight. A methadone client is an example of an outpatient.

Physical Dependence—the physiological need that opiate addicts develop over time for heroin or other opiates.

Pimp—a person who procures prostitutes for customers and solicits customers for prostitutes.

Prostitute—a person who engages in sexual activity in exchange for money or drugs.

Pseudo-Cop—a reference to the authoritarian role that methadone counselors sometimes feel compelled to play with methadone clients.

Rational Recovery—an alternative movement, or a separate branch of the Recovery Movement, that espouses tenets quite different from those of AA about the best ways to achieve sobriety.

Reality Check—a therapeutic technique in which the counselor reminds the client of certain indisputable facts in order to help the client maintain a reality-based perception of the world.

Recovery—the achievement of sobriety along with a commitment to ongoing sobriety.

The Recovery Movement—an organized group of addicts who support one another in their efforts to achieve and maintain lasting sobriety. The best-known representative group of the Recovery Movement is Alcoholics Anonymous, or AA.

Relapse—the tendency of addicts who have stopped using drugs to resume using drugs one or more times before achieving lasting sobriety.

Repetition Compulsion—a Freudian term used to describe a deep-rooted, trauma-based tendency to stay stuck in a destructive behavioral pattern. For instance, a child of an alcoholic parent may repeat his or her childhood traumas by growing up to marry an alcoholic.

Residential Substance Abuse Treatment—intensive inpatient drug treatment that takes place over the course of several weeks or months within the confines of a hospital or other treatment facility.

Resistant—a term used to describe a client who is emotionally inert and reluctant to make difficult changes.

Rush—the burst of euphoria that is experienced almost immediately after injecting heroin. The rush is usually followed by a period of semi-consciousness known as "nodding out."

Scattered-Site Treatment Model—a treatment model that would allow LAAM clients to dose in doctors' offices scattered throughout the area rather than at a single, centralized clinic.

Schizophrenia—a severe psychotic disorder characterized by a variety of features, including delusions, auditory or visual hallucinations, loose associations, and disorganized speech patterns.

Scoring or Copping—slang terms for buying or otherwise acquiring illegal drugs.

Self-Medicating—the tendency of addicts to abuse drugs in order to numb or anesthetize themselves as a means of avoiding emotional pain.

Shooting Up—slang for intravenously using narcotic substances, such as heroin.

Snorting—slang for nasally inhaling powdered narcotic substances, such as heroin.

Sobriety—prolonged abstinence from licit and/or illicit substances.

Spilling—the act of revealing one's most innermost feelings in a "flooding" fashion.

Strung Out—slang used to describe someone who is deeply involved in drug abuse, and is therefore in very poor physical and emotional health.

Substitute Addiction—the replacement of one habit-forming behavior (such as drug use) with another (such as compulsive sex or shoplifting).

Supervision—clinical guidance and wisdom imparted from an experienced clinician to a novice during regularly scheduled meetings.

Syringe—an implement used for injecting liquids into the body.

Take-Home Dose—a small container of methadone mixed with juice that a compliant client is given by methadone clinic staff to refrigerate and ingest in the comfort of home.

Thanatos—the ancient Greek god of death and destruction.

Transference—the vast range of feelings that counselors inspire in their clients.

Traumatization—prolonged suffering as a result of repeated or continuous bodily or psychological injury.

Triggers—environmental cues—persons, places, or things—that cause addicts to crave or use illicit drugs.

Unconditional Positive Regard—a therapeutic technique whereby a counselor gives clients a steady flow of encouragement and positive feedback.

Urinalysis—laboratory analysis of clients' urine to check for the presence of illicit substances, such as heroin or cocaine.

Urine Technician—a person whose job it is to monitor methadone clients as they urinate into containers for laboratory analysis.

Vicarious Traumatization—a potent form of countertransference in which counselors feel injured or "traumatized" as a result of working with large numbers of clients who have been victimized.

War Stories—the painful anecdotes about their drug-abusing days that recovering addicts and alcoholics share in AA and NA meetings to remind themselves and each other of how unmanageable their lives were when they were actively using drugs.

Withdrawal—the painful period following discontinued use of a licit or illicit drug marked by excruciating physiological and psychological symptoms, including nausea, diarrhea, and excessive perspiration.

Works—the various tools—spoon, tourniquet, lighter, and syringe—that comprise an intravenous heroin addict's drug-using paraphernalia.

Index

About the Author

Rachel Greene Baldino, MSW, LCSW, was born in northern California and grew up in Iowa and upstate New York. She received her bachelor's degree from the State University of New York at Albany and her master's degree from the Boston College Graduate School of Social Work. She has worked as a substance abuse counselor at a methadone clinic. Her articles have appeared in *The New Social Worker*, and she currently serves as a member of that publication's editorial advisory board. She lives with her husband in Massachusetts.

Other Social Work Publications from White Hat Communications...

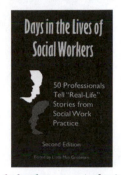

THE SOCIAL WORKER'S INTERNET HANDBOOK

by Gary B. Grant and Linda May Grobman

"engaging and thorough....
should be in all academic libraries."
LIBRARY JOURNAL, October 1, 1998

"It's great! Lots of neat resources, plain language, tips, and touts...
great basic book for anybody's undergraduate/graduate library!!!"
Ogden Rogers, Ph.D., ACSW
BSW Program Director, University of Wisconsin-River Falls
Listowner, SOCWORK Internet Mailing List

Thousands of social workers are using the Internet to connect with colleagues, find information to use in their work with clients, and provide services and information. You can, too.

Read this book and learn how you can:
- **Connect** to the Internet
- **Choose** an Internet Service Provider
- **Use** mailing lists and newsgroups
- **Surf** the World Wide Web
- **Network** with social work colleagues from around the world
- **Find** helpful information and resources for your clients
- **Advocate** online for your favorite causes
- **Raise funds** for your organization or agency using the Internet
- **Search** online for a social work job
- **Provide** a community service by creating your own Web page.

You will also find important information about the ethical concerns surrounding electronic communication and provision of online social work services.

PLUS...Reviews of over 350 Web Sites of Interest to Social Workers, Glossary, Index, and Additional Reading Resources

ISBN: 0-9653653-5-2   1998   Price: $24.95 (U.S.)
Shipping/Handling: $3.50/U.S. addresses; $6/Canada; $12/outside U.S. and Canada
240 pages   8 1/2 x 11   Softcover

Order from White Hat Communications, P.O. Box 5390, Harrisburg, PA
17110-0390 with order form in the back of this book.

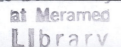

GUIDE TO SELECTING AND APPLYING TO MASTER OF SOCIAL WORK PROGRAMS–4th EDITION

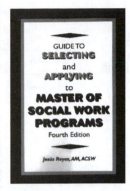

GUIDE TO
SELECTING
and
APPLYING
to
**MASTER OF
SOCIAL WORK
PROGRAMS**
Fourth Edition

Jesús Reyes, AM, ACSW

Required reading for anyone who wants to get a master's degree in social work.

A former admissions officer tells you what to look for in schools, and what schools are looking for in applicants!

In the *Guide to Selecting and Applying to MSW Programs, 4th Edition,* you will learn about the admissions process from an insider's perspective. You will discover what will help (and hurt) your chances of being accepted to the school of your choice, and you will find tips on deciding which school is right for you.

You should read this book to find out:

- What factors to consider when determining your **interest** in a school of social work
- What **admissions committees** look for in an applicant
- Whether your **GPA** and **test scores** matter
- How to gain social work related **experience** that will help in the application process
- Who to ask for **letters of reference** (and who not to ask)
- What to include in the **personal essay or biographical statement**
- Which schools are **accredited** by the Council on Social Work Education, and why this is important
- Where to find out about social work **licensing** in each state.

Jesús Reyes, AM, ACSW, *is Director of the Social Service Department of the Circuit Court of Cook County, IL. Formerly Assistant Dean for Enrollment and Placement at the University of Chicago School of Social Service Administration, he has reviewed many graduate school applications and has advised numerous applicants.*

ISBN: 1-929109-01-6. 252 pages. $19.95 (U.S. funds)
Shipping/Handling: $3.50/U.S. addresses; $6/Canada; $12/outside U.S. and Canada. **In Pennsylvania, add 6% sales tax.**

Order from White Hat Communications, P.O. Box 5390, Harrisburg, PA 17110-0390 with order form in the back of this book.

ORDER FORM

I would like to order the following social work publications from White Hat Communications:

Qty.	Item	Price
_____	Days in the Lives of Social Workers @ $17.95	_____
_____	Social Worker's Internet Handbook @ $24.95	_____
_____	Guide to Selecting/Applying to MSW @ $19.95	_____
_____	Welcome to Methadonia @ $15.95	_____
_____	New Social Worker Subscription (see rates on a previous page)	_____

Please send my order to:

Name _____

Organization _____

Address _____

City_____ State____ Zip _____

Telephone _____

Please send me more information about ❑social work and ❑non-profit management publications available from White Hat Communications.

Sales tax: Please add 6% sales tax for books shipped to Pennsylvania addresses.

Shipping/handling:
❑Books sent to U.S. addresses: $3.50 first book/$1 each add'l book.
❑Books sent to Canada: $6.00 per book.
❑Books sent to addresses outside the U.S. and Canada: $12.00 per book.

Payment:
Check or money order enclosed for $_____
U.S. funds only.

Please charge my: ❑Mastercard ❑Visa

Card #: _____

Name on card: _____

Billing address (if different from above): _____

_____

Signature: _____

Mail this form with payment to:
WHITE HAT COMMUNICATIONS, P.O. Box 5390, Dept. WM
Harrisburg, PA 17110-0390
Credit card orders may be called to 717-238-3787
or faxed to 717-238-2090
or order online at http://www.socialworker.com